Removing

The

Fr♥gments

A Healing Journey Through the Pieces of a Broken Heart Story

Ifedayo Greenway

& 11 Women Healed by the Heart of the Matter

REMOVING THE FRAGMENTS

Printed in the United States of America

ISBN: 979-8-9868570-5-3

Ifedayo is available for speaking engagements, book signings, and workshops. Send your requests to ifegreenway@igandmore.com

Special discounts are available on bulk quantity purchases by book clubs, associations and special interests groups. For more details email: ifegreenway@igandmore.com

This book is dedicated to the hearts that
are yearning to heal.

God made my life complete when I placed
all the pieces before Him

Psalm 18:20 (MSG)

Foreword

Monique Jewell Anderson

I remember the night well when Frank proposed marriage to me. We were at a ministry conference, and the theme was family restoration. Three months later, we were hitched, and I had to do something I had never done before, move to another state. I was all for traveling the world and having new experiences with my Army husband just as long as he promised to bring me back home when he retired. And he promised just that. As a new military spouse, I quickly realized moving came with the territory, and it happened every three years. Frank and I moved from Virginia to Raleigh North Carolina, to San Pedro California, to Baumholder Germany, to Ft. Monmouth New Jersey, and finally, back to Virginia. What made moving so interesting was I always got a sense when it was time to move to the next location. As a mom of five with a husband who could deploy at a moment's notice, planning was necessary and crucial. So, when I knew we had new PCS orders, I started cleaning house, literally. My rule of thumb was if it was still in a box from the last move, it had to go.

One such moment happened on our move from San Pedro to Germany. I was on a stool in the kitchen, and I handed Frank a few of his Army beer mugs and said, "these are trash." I said it so fast because I was on a mission; we had movers coming to pack us up soon. A few minutes later, I saw the mugs still on the cabinet and thought he must've forgotten. So, I picked one up, and just as I was about to throw it away, Frank interjected, "No! I want to keep those."

I snapped, "Man, throw them things away. You don't even drink beer; no one does, so why keep them?"

"That's not the point. They're sentimental. They represent my previous battalions." As a young Army officer, Frank pointed to certain emblems on each mug and went down memory lane. I saw how his eyes lit up, and the rhythm of his voice slowed and sped up with each recall. Then, I got it. To me, they were irrelevant, but to him, they were precious and keepsakes.

We did this dance for years when we had to move. With every relocation, the family had more things and treasures they wanted to keep; however, although our family size had changed, my process had not. I enjoyed throwing things away that no longer served a purpose. I needed the move to be smooth, and I'd have fewer things to unpack at our new home. Most times, the hubby had to work, and the kids would be in school, so that left me home alone with boxes on top of boxes. So, as in any marriage, sometimes we agreed on what was to go, and other times we agreed to disagree.

We all have boxes – large and small, opened and unopened. And for the purpose of this particular writing, they represent fragments. Over time, we have collected little pieces of ourselves that we keep, hide, or forget about – until we move. It's not until life forces us to see the box and deal with the contents that it causes us to shift and become uncomfortable. This movement can be emotional, psychological, financial, and a host of other things. But whatever the box is, it must be dealt with. Unfortunately, more often than not, we tuck the boxes that have lies, shame, and guilt under our beds or in our closets and ignore them. Again, until we move.

Movement is the act of changing physical location or position, a change or development. I gotta be honest; this is when my flesh wants to cuss. We all know where our boxes are, and they are just fine where we have them. And, as my neck rolls, when I want to deal with them, I will. But no! God really does want what's best for me…and you.

For months, I have sat with the women of this anthology. Not only have I seen their tears, but the Lord and I have also been the cause of them. And what they all have in common is this: no one wanted to open their box...but they did. They took out its contents, the fragments, the scars, the lies, the judgments, the painful memories, one by one. They examined them under the guidance and comfort of Holy Spirit. They bit their tongues when they, too, wanted to cuss. They snatched their edges, threw their shoes off, and got on their knees and bellies and howled. One by one, they pulled and wrestled with God for their truths. Instead of ignoring them for a second longer, they recognized their once-cherished fragments and embraced them with all they had.

Then a wonderful and glorious thing happened. They got strong enough to remove some things from their lives. They removed strongholds, fears, insecurities, low self-esteem, and generational curses. They found the freedom to speak up for themselves. They felt their help coming on with every word written as they exposed God's truth in the lies the enemy told about them. They got their fight back! And now they are free, healed, and delivered. But what they are not is naïve. There will be more boxes, other fragments, and more moves. But oh baby, these women are locked and loaded with new strategies and unbeatable weapons. You talk'in about courage? These ladies talked their talk and walked their walk.

As you turn the pages of their lives, I pray you will get the unction to pray until mountains crumble and demons flee. I pray you will speak into existence the good things our God has in store for you. As you read about the tenacity and resilience of these women, I pray you will see yourself in them and know that you are not alone. For I decree and declare that your best days are ahead and that you are anointed to remove the fragments in your life.

Contents

Fragments of a Changing Heart

Ifedayo Greenway

I was preparing my presentation and talking points for my annual Change Experience event when I made what seemingly felt like a spiritual and emotional mishap by asking God for His help. "God, what do you want me to share with the women this year? How do you want me to approach this assignment for the maximum transformational impact? His response was, "Do it from your heart Dayo."

Those words prompted this writing journey and required me to perform an unplanned emotional EKG on the core cardiovascular organ responsible for flushing out my feelings.

The atmosphere in my office was ripe for a productive work session. The sun from daybreak was perfectly positioned in the window. My cup of fresh hot coffee was nearby in my favorite mug, and I had taken a few sips of it while listening to the inspirational words of a prolific speaker. After that, I turned on some instrumental worship music to help center my mind as I reflected on my morning motivation and moved from one task to another. And yet, without warning, those six words immediately suspended my efficiency and brought my efforts to a screeching halt. God's reply left me in an idle state of confusion as I stared at my computer screen.

To do something from my heart suggests there is a sincere and wholehearted effort in the execution of it. This was my seventh year doing the event, and I was sure that every year, my team and I put forth an unfeigned effort in the planning phases. But somehow, the Master's instruction hit differently. This to-do directive was deeper than looking for a venue, signing catering contracts, or leading planning and strategy sessions for an optimum experience; all of that had already been done. This mandate aligned with the Biblical principle, "Out of the abundance of the heart, the mouth speaks."

God wanted to test my heart to ensure I spoke life to the women when I opened my mouth. And in my mind, this was an unfair request because all four chambers were resting in the valley of the shadows of death.

With the recent events in my life, I had every reason to cancel The Change Experience and refund the attendees their registration fees. Still, I was committed to carrying out the assignment and showing up. But for God to ask me to find the inner strength to dig deep into a shallow space and convey something meaningful felt thoughtless and insensitive.

The Change Experience was scheduled for September 23 - 24, 2022. However, just eighteen days before that, my ex-husband and the father of my only daughter succumbed to his battle with ALS. We were in the throes of grieving. There was a gaping breach in my soul. I had spent days and nights rocking my daughter through her gut-wrenching moments. I didn't know my heart could feel the anguish it felt when she would cry out, "daddy." What used to be how she greeted her father when entering his presence was now a daunting plea to see him one last time. Clearly, I was operating from an emotional deficit. How could I be expected to utter powerful words and release a surplus?

As the host and a transformational coach, I would grace the platform every year with the same call and response. I'd say, "Yes, Yes," and the audience would holler back, "Yes, Change." The self-proclaimed mantra represented a determination to transition, transform, and heal. It was the persuasion to pursue the evolving door of transformative turns until it wasn't. I was tired of things changing, and deep down on this inside, the blood my fragmented heart was pumping screamed, "F*** change!"

I was resentful. God was not considering the timing of change, whether I was ready, whether I

3

could handle it, or even the fact that He had already altered so much in my life.

In August 2021, I released my memoir, The Pathway, The Journey, The Change. A few days after that, a close friend almost died from Covid. My oldest son, deployed in Kuwait, called with disturbing news. My youngest son, living in California, called that same day to tell me he was in a car accident. I was emotionally numb and despondent from all that was happening, and I demanded answers from God. "Why is all of this happening at the same time?" Finally, He said, "You released change in the atmosphere. You don't get to tell me how to do it." Whew... God ain't never lied. That was when I realized that as much as I wanted to control everything in my life, I had no say in this part of my change journey.

My ex-husband's death was the icing on the proverbial cake of a series of unplanned, unforeseen, and unwanted changes. It came riding in on the remnants of what felt like shattered dreams and broken promises from God. I heard someone say once that many things are breaking your heart before you even realize it's broken.

My life's modifications were not just about altering what I eat, shifting from place to place in my purpose journey, or even changing the people in my inner circle. This time, transformation came for new territory. It came for **everything** that was inflexible, every stagnant mindset, every condescending voice, and every bit of bitterness that I held towards God for His sovereignty. It came for my heart.

I wasn't ready. Truthfully, there were times when my "yes change" was contingent upon me being able to do it my way, on my terms, and in my timing. The idea of God reminding me that I don't get to tell Him how to make the necessary changes in my life was scary. Not being in control was unsettling as it felt like poignant pain was coming to the surface and demanding attention.

There's a story in the Bible about a shipwreck and how the survivors had to float to the shore on the broken piece to stay alive.

The heart of the matter is...

My life's ship had wrecked over and over again. I had been trying to stay alive and keep my head above water. I was floating on remnants and broken pieces for longer than I care to admit. The shore always felt so far away. In fact, it felt like the tiny remains I was floating on were breaking into smaller pieces of debris. Transformation was no longer something I easily celebrated. Rather, it felt like a reactive survival exercise of rummaging through the piled-on wreckage of seemingly broken promises from God.

5

I had a covenant with God. We had a mutual agreement, and we'd made some promises to each other. My hope was anchored in the fact that if I did my part, He would do His. My assurance was in the scripture Psalm 37:4, which says, "if you delight yourself in the Lord (my part), then He will give you the desires of your heart (His part)." But the continual breakage suggested that God had abandoned our pact. I was angry with Him, and my familiar run-ins with change had definitely led me into a dark place of contempt.

God! Hadn't I done enough for you to at least give me some of the desires of my heart? Haven't I earned a return on my "delight in change" investment? Walking in my purpose was not giving me back what I was putting in. I want a husband. I want my business to prosper to leave a stream of wealth for my children. I want a house - I did everything I was told to prepare for one, and somehow the loan still fell through. I want to not have to fight so hard for promises you seem so freely handing out to others who don't even seem to be in covenant with you. And for God's sake, I wanted my daughter's father to LIVE so badly! I would have given up anything I've ever asked you for if you would've just let him live to see her graduate from high school and college and walk her down the aisle of matrimony. He was not just her father; he was my friend, my partner in parenting, and a man I once

6

loved. We were divorced. We had encountered good times, bad times, and trials in raising our daughter and even tested the thin line between love and hate. But through it all, we had a friendship connection - and that meant that even as his ex-wife, I was there until death did us part.

Recently I read a book titled Good Boundaries and Goodbyes by Lysa Terkeurst, in which one of the chapters is called, A Million Little Funerals. In this chapter, she shares the brilliant strategy of performing unconventional "funerals" as a way of standing firm on relational boundaries and marking moments of emotional closure.

She speaks to the possibility of taking a break for a season of healing without fully breaking ties with a person. Well, the biggest change in my life, the one that took the most out of me and rocked the innermost core of my being, was this was no break. It wasn't like the moments my ex-husband, and I had in the past, where we would frustrate one another, go off and heal, then come back to the parenting table. His death was a final and forever goodbye! The funeral was REAL. Sitting in that chapel on September 12, 2022 (just one day from the date of our marriage ceremony 18 years prior) was a tangible and irreversible experience that impacted the rhythmic beats of my organ. I would miss him just as much as my daughter did. And saying goodbye to him left my heart in need of resuscitation.

Why was God not giving me any of the desires of my heart? Why had I worked so much to heal, and my heart was still in pieces? Why had He delayed or denied me so many things? In a season where I was expecting something from Him, why was He still taking so much away from me?

The weight of my emotions had taken a toll. With so much fragmentation, I was gently forced (by my doctor) into taking a sabbatical. I spent weeks trying to decipher the emotional destruction I was left with. My questions pulled back the layers of the heart of the matter, ultimately leading me to the truth of the matter.

My mentor, editor, and friend challenged me with a thought-provoking perspective pertinent to my healing journey. She asked, "Did death happen to your life or in your life?"

And what I've come to learn is this…when I process pain as a compilation of things happening to my life, I rest comfortably in the extent of despair that makes me a constant victim. But when I dance with the idea that things are happening in my life, I accept that change is the very nature of life itself and measure myself accordingly. I steward the pieces differently and affirm that I was built to withstand the natural proclivity of being gracefully broken.

An Automatic External Defibrillator (AED) analyzes the heart rhythm. Then, it delivers an electric shock to restore it to a normal flow. That day sitting at my desk, I was forced to evaluate the particles left behind from broken heart stories - those things that could be responsible for my destiny's demise. I was in emotional and spiritual cardiac arrest. God was using His own devices to perform CPR so that He could restore a healthy cadence in my heart. What felt like an unfair request was a life-saving encounter.

In that bible story that I mentioned earlier, remember I said the survivors used the pieces of the ship to get them safely to the shore? Well, that says to me that fragments, if addressed and used properly, will be the very thing that saves my life, although the shipwreck was initially designed to take it. Unfortunately, I was not using the fragments properly. I focused too much on their origins rather than how God wanted me to use them to move forward. I focused on the breakage and not the value of the pieces.

There are two types of promises in the Bible: conditional and unconditional. The scripture I had been holding God accountable to (Him giving me the desires of my heart) was conditional. But in reality, I had a role I was not completely fulfilling. I was screaming, "yes, change," hoping that if I made enough changes my way, I would drown out the

9

demands of change that God wanted me to do his way. But, instead, he required something from me that I had not yet given Him - my whole heart!

I was making that scripture about things, people, and success stories. God's plea was that in all things, HE would become my one and true desire. I was blaming God for not giving me what I wanted, and His heart was grieved that He was not the thing I longed for the most.

The truth of the matter is it was time for me to relinquish the pain of letting go of the big thing and focus on the seemingly little things that were left behind. What felt like breakage is now the thing I know I must grab on to and accept that it's taking me to my final destination. Yet, every broken fragment is drawing me closer to God. And my heart will forever be changing as I embrace the idea of completely placing it in the hands of the one who loves me the most.

At The Change Experience, when it was my turn to speak, I had no choice but to do it from my heart, broken and all. My moments of transparency not only shifted us into an atmosphere of alleviating pain but also compelled eleven other women to heal as they got to the heart of the matter in their transformational stories.

We have emptied our hearts of some raw emotions towards life, loss, others, ourselves, and even God. We removed the faces of counterfeit perfection and the fear of judgment from others for baring our souls.

Our tears were plentiful. Our journeys were not indicative of climbing crystal stairs. And a lot of what we thought, spoke, and wrote during challenging times in our lives would never check the box for being "religiously correct" - but we didn't back down from authenticity. We trusted God to handle the good, the bad, and the absolute ugliest crevices of our pain. We refused to give up - we declared that we would keep writing until He healed us.

So, from our mended arteries to your broken vessels - from our healed hearts to your hurting heart, know this...

Coming out of the storm does not negate the aftermath. Could you imagine if we experienced a hurricane or tornado and tried to move on without cleaning up the debris?

Survival is not healing. You absolutely have the right to celebrate making it through - but you also have the responsibility to address the pieces left behind from the life events that activated survival mode.

It's time for you to HEAL! And you get to do it without regard for what others think about your process.

Let's go to work! Let's dive into the stories of the other eleven courageous women. Let's Remove the Fragments.

Oh, and you know I couldn't end this chapter without saying it one last time. But this time, when I say it, I mean it more than ever! This time, I can scream it from the mountaintop without fear of an avalanche or fractured mass of emotions overtaking my soul. I can let it boldly roar from my core because **this time** it speaks to the wholeness of my heart rather than just the fragmented pieces. **Yes, Yes. YES CHANGE!**

Fragments of a Weighted Heart

Jada D. Thompson

"I don't want to serve you! I don't want the gift or anointing you put on my life. I don't want to preach, and I don't want to mime. You don't deserve to be applauded or glorified when you caused me this much anguish. I HATE YOU!"

Truth be told, God received a lot of fuck you's the first year I was fatherless. The aching was so unbearable it caused my nerves to go numb. The world was moving way too fast around me, and all I wanted was for it to slow down so I could catch up and understand what was happening to my life. Honestly, I thought serving God would be all peaches and cream. After attending church every Wednesday and Sunday, I only knew Him to be a good, good Father. However, when I viewed my father in his casket, I questioned my belief and faith in HIM.

If Abba Father was so good, why did HE hurt me? I know I am not perfect, but I didn't deserve to be 17 with no daddy. That wasn't supposed to be a part of my testimony. Spiritually, I was broken. I did not know what to pray for myself. Instead, I took on

13

the responsibility of my dead daddy and consistently prayed for my mother and little sister. I didn't want God to do anything for me because He had messed up big time. Mentally, my head was all over the place. I was a senior in high school trying to understand how I could do schoolwork, apply for colleges, and grieve all at the same time. The world didn't decelerate or show any mercy even though I pulled as hard as I could on the emergency brake of life. I just needed a moment; to realize what was accurately happening in my life. Emotionally, I checked out. I refused to allow any feelings to penetrate my heart, and my tear ducts became paralyzed. As my anger went unresolved, I chose bitterness. And walked around with a mask to hide my true grief and sadness. I didn't know anyone who could help me while also understanding me, so I shut everyone out.

Two hours before my dad died, he dropped me off at school and told me he would be back later to pick me up. I got out of the car, rushing to class because I was late, and I didn't say, "I love you." Neglecting to utter those three words caused me to shatter into fragments as the months and years went on. This is one of my biggest regrets. How could I be rude enough to leave the car and not tell my father I loved him? How was I so self-absorbed that I missed my last opportunity to express my love to him? Time and time again, I beat myself up for not telling him. And while my mother told me he knew I loved him, that wasn't enough for me. I wanted another chance with him. I not only wanted to say it, but I wanted to hear it back.

My dad and I were thick as thieves for the first four years and ten months of my life, but that all changed when I was no longer his youngest baby. I was pissed when I lost my father's undivided attention. The week before his passing, I thought we had a chance to go back to the way it used to be. I thought I had time for us to get to know each other again. However, the Omniscient Father took him before that could happen. If the God I confessed to loving sees and knows all, then He knew my heart better than I even knew my own. The issue I had with God, however, was He knew we were getting closer, and our relationship was getting better, but He confiscated my daddy anyway. So I had to reconcile my biological dad's absence with the disappointment caused by my heavenly dad.

I don't know why I did; I just did. I leaned into the massive responsibility of being a caregiver. I placed the burden of my family's grieving world on my shoulders. Without hesitation, I picked up the pieces for my mother and sister so they could keep living, even if that meant I had to stop. Even with the weight of their tears, angst, and the daily unknowns being far too heavy for me to bare, that didn't stop me from trying. And I was going to do it without

God's help. Frankly, because I didn't trust God not to drop the ball again.

After finishing high school, I went to college full-time. I went to class every day and home every weekend. I consumed myself with becoming my sister's mother, my mother's mother, and my mother's mini-husband. I felt I needed to pick up the slack as the years passed. I got the cars serviced, made sure the state inspections were up to date, fixed the toilets, put up blinds, put furniture together, or dismantled furniture, and used my refund checks to help keep a roof over our heads. I already had anger issues and having to bury my father before he saw me graduate high school or college, buy my first car, walk down the aisle with me, preach my first sermon, teach my first mime class, or give him a grandchild caused my anger issues to drastically increase. He was gone, and I was furious with God for putting me in this mess. How could thè Father take my father?

Having a surviving parent is not for the weak. As conversations continued in my family, I realized just how much I was misunderstood and how my feelings simply didn't matter. Sometimes, I felt like my mother's grief competed with mine. I felt like her grief of losing a husband trumped the grief of daddy's little girl. So, I fought diligently to be seen, and if that meant I became a people pleaser while fighting, then so be it. I couldn't bear the thought of losing another parent, so I sacrificed myself, my feelings, and my personal decisions. Nevertheless, while working so hard to be seen and understood, and as the caregiver, I was taken for granted. My decision to handle the responsibilities of someone else's household came back to bite me in the ass. The small fragments of resentment and bitterness began to turn into bigger shards. My shattered heart started to slice up and damage the other chambers that still desperately needed mending.

The new fragments of my being began to irritate my old ones. Although young in years, I had already endured so much before this, and still, life's twists and turns came like a well-trained UFC fighter. I had been raped, molested, and struggled with finding my identity. Losing my daddy was just too much. Growing up in church, I heard about this loving and merciful God that was everywhere. Yet, I felt alone, abandoned, and abused. There was no way God loved my family and me. This was not love; it couldn't be. Love isn't supposed to hurt, is it? With each powerful blow that life threw at me landing as a potentially fatal gut punch, my only options were to tap out or die trying.

The state I was in was horrific. I knew I was spiraling out of control when sleeping with men, smoking weed, and being my mother's personal trash can were my crutch. How could multiple men, mind-

17

altering cannabis, and being a decorated garbage disposal be things I lean on for support? The men got five minutes of fame, my old plug got his money, and my mother got her so-called freedom. However, I was left unsatisfied, broke, and emotionally incarcerated. The scabs on my soul that I constantly picked at became infected. That one hole in my heart that my dad left became countless more. My spirit was decaying, and I was disgusted with life.

The heart of the matter is...

I had no choice but to run back to God.

One night as I was taking a shower, I began to weep. I saw pieces of my body plummet at my feet like a shattered mirror. I heard God sternly but calmly say, "Daughter, this time, the temporary adhesive you use won't put you back together." My days as a superhero were over, and it was time to retire my cape. Unhealthy grief caused me to have short-term memory loss of who I was and who I was called to be. I allowed men to get the most expensive entrée on the menu at an outrageous discounted rate. I allowed myself to overdose on blunts just to take a recess on life. I allowed someone I would give my life to abuse my generous acts of service to make themselves feel better. I knew I could no longer place other feelings before my own.

In the time of processing everything my weighted heart had encountered, God exposed to me my role of trying to be him. I worked hard to control my family and my grieving world, but how can I control something I didn't create, mold, shape, or orchestrate? I caused more damage trying to be Him than allowing God to be Himself. God had to force me out of His position by allowing friction between my mother and me. The only way God could get me to resign was to allow heart-wrenching conversations between us to happen. Just like my heart has fragments, hers does too. The truth is, my mother loves me and would do anything for me. Since the day I was born, she has called me her sunshine, and that will never change. I had to realize that God was only breaking my weighted heart gracefully to allow total healing to take place. I became lost in helping everyone that I didn't receive help from anyone. Pride overtook me, and without realizing what I was doing, I thought I could be just like God and not need assistance. I was wrong and had to repent for my actions. Being broken and weighed down did not feel good. My last option was to place all the fragments before God so I could be complete again (Psalm 18:20).

God didn't abandon me; I wanted him to just so I could throw it back in his face. It's been 1,982 days without having my daddy. And every day, with no breaks, God has picked me up, carried me, laid with me, stood with me, and didn't leave me for nothing. Even when I did not acknowledge him there. My testimony is that after my father's death, I had someone who willingly wanted to step in and be whatever I needed during every wave of my grieving stages. I did leave him, though. I walked away from God out of fear, frustration, and fatigue. My expectation was for God to always fix my fragmented heart, not be the cause of it. My mistake was not trusting the same God who allowed my heart to suffer from loss, the elegance to grieve. It was in His plan to immediately captivate my heart. In the same cadence as my father's last breath, God was ready to step in and step up to fulfill the void in my soul. Yet, it was my calling to accept his invitation.

From my healed heart to your hurting heart...

The fragments of a weighted heart are sharp broken wedges of me that caused damage to the healthier parts of me. Even when I thought the finest of wedges couldn't be broken down anymore, they seemed to weaken even more. I had to apologize to my heart for putting other hearts before it. I didn't protect or pay the well-needed attention to the very thing that pumps blood to my other organs. I ignored the signs my soul publicized due to my pride. Today and forevermore, I vow to choose my heart strings, my heart chambers, and vessels over the thoughts and feelings of other people. This time around, I'll allow

God to be my cardiovascular surgeon and put a muzzle on my fear. It's impossible for the surgery to go wrong when the medical practitioner qualified to practice surgery is the potter. My heart is no foreign clay to God's hands.

Fragments of a Silenced Heart

Sandra L. Parker

"Whatever concerns me, concerns God." I lived by this phrase for years. It's a part of my bio that gets a smile and a nod of approval when people hear or read it. It is not just a catchy slogan but a true expression of how I believed God carried me no matter what. I repeat this expression whenever I'm trying to find a parking space on the front row at the mall or looking for the holy ghost price of my favorite item in the grocery store. It may appear a little extreme to some, but it's a simple yet powerful motto that has gotten me through torrential storms. The evidence of such a short slogan has been so great that some of my friends have adopted it in their lives. When doubt consumed me, it offered me so much hope, especially in those moments. These five little words inspired me to keep going when I wanted to give up. I was convinced that God cared about everything that mattered to me, too. Until one day, I wasn't so sure.

I woke up with a strong feeling of just being overwhelmed. After a quick survey of my life, I concluded that every area seemed to be falling apart. Sitting on the edge of my bed, I could only muster enough strength to shake my head. I couldn't believe that my life had come to this. I tried to find the good, but there was nothing. Yeah, I was breathing, but at the moment, that wasn't enough to be grateful for. Instead, I was angry and infuriated with God. Where the hell was He? When did He stop caring? This damn sure can't be the hope and future He promised me? As the silence enveloped the room and my resentment towards God increased, my tears fell.

When I think of fragments, I immediately see broken pieces. My mind reverts to when I dropped a glass on the kitchen floor, which shattered into a million pieces. At that moment, the current state of my life flashed in front of me. Those little pieces represented my life. They were the fragments that caused my disdain toward God. Crushed dreams. A broken heart. Crumbled hopes. Cracked desires. A fractured purpose. Much like the glass could hold me responsible for being careless and allowing it to fall, I blamed God for the current state of my life. It was how I saw God handle me, and it pissed me off to the point that I silenced my heart.

I immediately shut down whenever I feel ignored or my feelings are being toyed with. It's a defense mechanism that doesn't always serve me well, but it's my safe space. My heart has been damaged enough

23

throughout the years, so removing myself from situations when I sense foul play is involved doesn't take much. So when it seemed as if God wasn't interested in playing fair, I did what I knew best, and that was to shut down and become silent.

My heart grew weary. I silenced God because it seemed like every desire I've ever had; he told me no. It was like God got a kick from seeing me find my way. It was one disappointment after another. I see others prosper, but I'm still in the same space. How many times do I have to witness the overflow in someone else's life?

I've spent countless hours making my requests known to God. Prayer has always been my saving grace because I could count on God to answer me, even if I didn't like His responses. I wasn't necessarily a prayer warrior, but I was good at getting my prayers to God. So, imagine my angst when my prayers seemed to fall on deaf ears.

My God-given purpose concerns me, and I would think it's on God's mind, too, right? But waking up feeling purposeless is incredibly aggravating. It's even more annoying to pray for direction, and there's no response. I didn't think God intended me to live a life of painful drudgery, but it's exactly what happened. I've even had the audacity to pray for a Godly relationship after being divorced and heartbroken more than anyone deserves. However,

I'm still single after 16 years. I consciously decided to trust God for the abundance and overflow He clearly says is mine. Still, somehow Peter gets robbed to pay Paul every payday. God's lack of response has affected me in the worst way.

I hear myself screaming, "God, I don't know what you want from me. I'm tired of unanswered prayers, and I'm done. I really don't want to hear anything else you have to say. I'm fed up with hoping and believing only to face another hurdle." I can relate to Sophia in The Color Purple when she said, "All my life, I had to fight!" I needed God to take the chokehold off me and allow me to really breathe. There was no fight left in me. I'm burned out, worn out, and depleted. If God had only told me what to do, I would have listened. It was as if He left me to figure things out on my own without leaving me His contact information. The bouts of trauma caused my faith to waver and left me speechless. In the absence of words, I adopted a new mantra, "I have nothing to say."

Someone recently told me, "Silence is when God has chosen not to speak, and silenced is when you have chosen to no longer listen to God." Her follow-up question rocked me in a way that I hadn't expected. In a calm but bold demeanor, she said, "Which is it for you?" As I wept, I quietly responded, "I have silenced God." I was floored by the direction of our conversation. Still, it presented a challenge to seek God in a manner that was scary and unfamiliar.

Over the next several days, I replayed our talk in my mind. It was undeniably a God moment and one that could not be ignored. Then, out of my mouth, I made a confession that could never be taken back. The truth is that I had silenced God out of anger, and it was now time for me to either put up or shut up. God and I had a score to settle, but it required me to speak to Him even when my mind tried to persuade me to remain silenced. Eventually, I convinced myself that the time was now.

In a fragile and vulnerable state, I cried out to God. Then, with nothing left to lose, I simply said to Him, "If you don't show up right now, I'm done." There are no other options; you have to come through for me. If I'm honest, I didn't even know what I expected from God. I didn't know what showing up for me really meant, nor did I have a clue as to what I was really seeking from Him. Yet, as angry as I had been with God, I was certain in that very moment that my desperation for help outweighed the anger I felt towards Him.

I would love to tell you that God responded swiftly, and our relationship has been fully restored. But that would be a lie. What I can say is that God heard me, and in spite of the pain and feelings of hopelessness and weakness I've endured, I'm convinced that God has not forgotten about me. Instead, he chose to remain silent on purpose. While I expected a distinct and audible voice, He needed me to trust that His daily whispers alone were just as powerful. It was the still, small voice that represented God's longing for intimacy just between the two of us.

The heart of the matter is...

Silencing God prevented me from seeing the better I had been praying and asking for all along. While I pleaded with God to improve my situation, my silenced heart caused an opportunity for me to draw strength from His power. As I begged God to resuscitate my circumstances, His goal was to ultimately resurrect my mindset instead. In the quiet moments, God was speaking, but I had turned a deaf ear to Him. My life was full of noise, and God was simply waiting for His turn to speak. His goal was to mold my life in such a way that would make me pliable enough to help others Speak life into their own situations.

What has resonated with me the most is that perspective is important. Cambridge dictionary defines perspective as "a particular way of considering something or thinking about a situation or problem in a wise and reasonable way." In essence, it's my ability to make a conscious decision to feel better about what's not better. Have I gotten a better job? No. Has

Boaz found me? Not yet. Are my finances any different? No. In fact, they have been stretched even more. I no longer see God's silence as a form of rejection, but I deliberately seize those moments as an opportunity to listen more intently to His whispers. The past few months have been extremely hectic and exhausting, but God has been gracious. In a moment of transparency, I admit that much of my relationship with God has relied not only on feeling His presence but hearing His voice. So, I had to ask myself, what if the primary purpose of His silence is actually an opportunity for Him to hear from me.

From my healed heart to your hurting heart...

The truth is that my healing is still taking place. While I often pray that God would increase His turnaround time in answering my prayers, I now understand that God's silence is one of His greatest tools for cultivating my dependence on Him.

Whenever you feel that God is not speaking, keep talking to Him. Instead of thinking of His silence as a license to turn your back on Him, I encourage you to see it as an invitation to change your perception and seek God even more diligently.

It's okay to be angry with God. But I employ you to not allow your heart to be silenced to the point that you miss the good things of God. Be wary of hardening yourself into responding with a heart that is silenced based on what you perceive as God ignoring you. You are not being overlooked or dismissed. The promise and promotion that you seek are coming. The desires of your heart will be manifested.

God's silence is not meant to punish or destroy you. Silence can be a reservoir of flowing peace, or it can be cold and sterile, a feeling of intentional abandonment. It's in the stillness that we have a choice to trust God or disregard His promise to never leave or forsake us. I am a living witness that not hearing God (especially when we think He should answer) sucks and sometimes leaves you tempted to throw in the towel. Don't give up in those moments but choose to dust yourself off and get back in the ring even if you have to crawl. Giving up is not an option. I won't promise that change will come overnight, and I won't give you false hope that there's pushing a magic button will force God to lift the silence just because we asked Him to. But beneath the doubts, emotional turmoil, trial and tribulation, every feeling of rejection, fear, doubt, and anger, if you listen closely enough, I promise that you may not hear God responding with words, but His power will be an inexhaustible flame that will shine a light in the dark places that concern you the most.

Fragments of a Guilty Heart

Felicia L. Vereen

As a young girl playing house was my favorite thing to do. I would gather my Barbie and Ken dolls and pretend they were getting married. We had a wedding ceremony and moved them into their beautiful Barbie house. As the old saying goes, first comes love, then comes marriage, then comes baby in the baby carriage. The life I wanted for my dolls was my dream, also. I believe every parent wants their child to meet their person, fall in love, get married, and have children. I'm sure my mom had the same dream for me.

I grew up to be a loving, responsible, intelligent, family-oriented woman. I promised myself I would not become a statistic; no, ma'am, that was not on my vision board. I planned to have a great career, marry a loving spouse then welcome a child into the world, or so I thought. So imagine my shock when this woman working in corporate America took a pregnancy test, and it was positive. I had no wedding ring on my finger and was humiliated. Stop it, Felicia; who are you fooling? When it came to this man, I was

30

dumb as a box of rocks, and I was not responsible at all. I was ashamed of being pregnant and not married. That's who I really was; I had become the statistic I never wanted to be.

I was a baby Momma. Me, Felicia, the church girl, the one who had it all together. So many thoughts ran through my mind. What would people think? Oh Lord, what would my church members say? How can I explain that I'm pregnant by a man I'm not married to or have a real relationship with? I was 32 years old; I should have known better. I was filled with so much guilt because, in my mind, I had started my baby girl's life behind the mark. She would not be raised by a mother and a father like I was. She'd go to school and see other kids with both parents and would not understand why she didn't have that in her household. I thought she would hate me for the choices that I had made for her. I was also embarrassed because this man I gave myself to did not want to be with me nor accept the responsibility of being the father of our child. That reality was more than I could handle at times.

My pregnancy was not a routine one. I had a medical condition that caused me to go into preterm labor. I remember going to a scheduled doctor's appointment and later being rushed to the emergency room to stop my labor. Three weeks later, my daughter was born 2 lbs. 9 oz. 19 inches long.

However, she had trouble breathing. The doctors immediately rushed her to NICCU for intubation. I didn't even get to hold her or see her face. I thought this was God trying to teach me a lesson. This was my punishment for having a baby out of wedlock. I cried in my hospital bed and constantly prayed that God would spare my child and punish me instead. I was so messed up in the head I thought God was punishing me through my baby girl.

The first day that I was able to see her precious face brought me overwhelming joy and anguish at the same time. My guilt made me think every medical issue she faced was my fault. It was my fault she was born prematurely; it was my fault she had a big tube shoved down her throat because she couldn't breathe on her own. It was my fault that she was born out of wedlock. I know being out of wedlock is not an issue in today's climate. As a church girl, I vowed to myself (and God) that I would be married before bringing children into this world. I was raised to believe children should be born to a husband and wife, a family. Anything outside of that was a sin in the eyes of God.

My daughter was three months early and stayed in the NICCU for another three months until she was healthy and ready to come home. We had a long road ahead of us. She went through a myriad of surgeries and procedures, and I was right there by her side. Her little body experienced so much, but she was my miracle baby. I lived in that hospital day and night, praying to God that she would be healthy and strong. During my visits, I saw fathers holding their babies with smiles as wide as the eye could see. I often wondered why I chose this person who did not love our child enough to show concern for her life. The guilt was sometimes overwhelming and made me feel like I had ruined her life.

Every day I asked God what I had done so bad to deserve such a fate. I often prayed and begged God to change her father's mind about us. I wanted him to soften his heart towards our daughter. I wanted him to see how beautiful our family could be and how much he needed us in his life. I wanted him to love us and to see our little family as an amazing gift from God. But I also asked God to make him love me. That's the part that broke my heart and made me feel the guiltiest. He did not love either of us and most of all, he didn't love me. It was tough to admit that I had been a fool for him.

I loved my daughter with every inch of my being. Still, I had been very irresponsible with this man, and now I was bringing her into this harsh world without a father. She would have no one to give her the daddy-daughter talks about boys. She would not be able to look at her dad as her superhero, thinking he was the smartest man in the world. All these things I wanted for her and more. But I had messed up because of my own selfishness. At a point in my life, I was only concerned with my needs. I was living life as if these types of things could not happen. I knew I could not blame her father for everything. It took two to make her.

I walked around smiling on the outside for others to see, but deep inside my heart, I felt like I had robbed my daughter of the life she deserved. A life with loving parents. I had a guilt-ridden heart. As her mother, I felt like I had to make up for him not being around; I often overcompensated for his absence. In my mind, I had to be mom and dad; I had to give her everything I thought she was missing. I had created a life that was sometimes stressful but thank God we had a great family and support system in place, and I was financially able to raise her to become a beautiful young girl.

The heart of the matter is...

While writing this chapter, I noticed I pointed a lot of fingers at my daughter's father. But I heard my conscience say it's time to look at yourself. After deep retrospection, I realized my guilty truth had nothing to do with my daughter and everything to do with me. So, 17-plus years later, I can finally be honest. I was angry, and I felt exposed. My secret was out – I was acting like I was following Gods word, but I was a woman having premarital sex. Even though I was embarrassed and humiliated, most of all, I was heartbroken. Yes, I was furious that her father chose not to be involved, loving, or financially responsible. But I was also disappointed because I allowed myself to have strong feelings for him, which he did not reciprocate. How dare this man treat me like I had no value and give up the opportunity to be the father of my child?

I was also ashamed, which made me feel guilty because I was old enough to know better. I wasn't a young girl; I was grown. I saw the signs that he wasn't the right man. I knew it wasn't the ideal situation, and I gave myself to him anyway without thinking about the repercussions. I never wanted to admit this to myself, so I chose to place the full blame on him and not look at my part as well. Now don't get me wrong, I still hold him accountable for not doing his part as a father. But at some point, I had to learn from my hard lessons.

I will admit it's been hard to sit down and review situations that did not go the way I designed. It is even harder to list why, but I am the type of woman who must understand the why to learn the great lesson in it all. So, when I was ready, I sat down to self-examine the circumstances. Upon doing so, I now understand that I cared about what people thought of me. I couldn't hide a baby; my gig was up, and they knew my secrets. I could no longer walk around perpetrating as if I had everything together and in order. I wanted the baby but didn't want to be a single mom. I felt used, and I wondered what was wrong with me. I was a good catch for any man, so why not this one? I was a mess. I felt rejected, alone, embarrassed, and punished. My self-esteem was at its lowest, and so was my heart.

After having a beautiful daughter, God taught me a powerful lesson. As I mentioned before, I felt ashamed, humiliated, and guilty. But I never stopped talking to God. After much prayer, I realized I am human. I am going to make mistakes, and life happens. I became less and less concerned with what people thought, and I focused on creating a wonderful life for my daughter and me. I had nothing to feel ashamed or humiliated about, I am not perfect, and yes, I have made some mistakes and will continue to make them. But I had no reason to feel guilty. God taught me that I can hold my head high amongst the best because I handled my responsibilities since the first day I carried her in my womb. He heard my prayers and comforted my heart, assuring me that my beautiful daughter would be okay. When I looked into her eyes for the first time, I felt God was right there with us, and I knew he had a plan for us. I promised her that she would have the best life I could offer and I would always be someone she could be proud to call mom.

I knew at that time; God had forgiven my guilty heart. He had restored a space in me, and I was open and willing to forgive myself. I am blessed to know that God forgives me for my wrongs. I know because he said all I had to do was repent and confess, and he would forgive me. If I still needed proof, all I had to do was open my eyes and see the amazing life he created for my daughter and me. God also showed me how it feels to be loved by a man. He taught me what to expect in a relationship and how to respond. He pointed out the characteristics I should look for in a man and, most importantly, that I need to see God in him. I need to see God in anyone I accept in my circle of love. Again, my daughter and I have a very loving family and friend support system. She has been blessed with a stepfather that treats her like his own. He doesn't like the word step; he considers himself her dad and showers her with abundant love daily.

The heart of the matter is my guilty heart played a terrible mind game on me; it had me thinking that something was wrong with me because this man didn't want a life with me. That I should be ashamed of myself because of my decisions along the way. That God was punishing me by sending me into premature labor. That I was a statistic, and I was less than because I was a single mother. I realized all those thoughts were false.

From my healed heart to your hurting heart...

Throughout this entire period of introspection, I learned three valuable lessons that I will remember forever. First, God is always with me, even when I make mistakes. Second, I should never care about the negative thoughts people may have of me as long as I strive to be my best version. Third, I should always respect myself. The true heart of the matter is my life experiences, whether good or bad, have helped to create the ambitious, strong, responsible, fierce, loving Christian woman and mother I am today.

Fragments of Santiago's Heart

Mavis G. Rowe

"Momma, who is my daddy, and why won't he visit me?"

"His name is Santiago Rivera, and he's married."

That was it, my introduction to my father. I was seven. My mom offered no other explanation, and at the time, that was cool with me. As long as I had a father, I was good…until I wasn't. My childhood was littered with his brief appearances, and as I got older, I felt the void. Finally, at ten, I asked to meet him, and through some secret maneuvering on my mother's part, I received a call from him one day after school. This stranger professed to be my dad. Our conversation was brief, exciting, and nerve-wracking. I assumed that now I had a real live person to attach to the stories of him, my life would change. He would be the dad I always wanted and expected to have, but I was wrong. He remained an enigma, only making appearances around my birthday, Christmas, and the beginning of the school year to give my mom monetary trinkets. However, his presence would forever be off-limits. I remained his little secret until I was 17, when my mother finally sought child support. Then I thought, Finally! He will acknowledge me to the world. But no, he kept his marriage intact, requested a paternity test, and continued to see me secretly. Over the years, that really pissed me off.

He constantly found ways to frustrate me. This turned to anger and then resentment. All while fueling my insecurity because I felt rejected. I envied the father-daughter relationships around me. It was the one thing I couldn't have or make him care enough to provide. So, I continued to stew in the juices of my emotions until I was exhausted. Someone needed to change, but not him. The change was with me.

Years ago, I was encouraged to reflect on that little seven-year-old girl and connect to her pain in therapy. The intense feelings still coursed through my body as I was asked, "What was the cause of her pain?" Wrath exploded from my mouth and heart as I thought about it. First, I was mad because I felt that he never cared about me. I had no proof that he did. We never talked or spent quality time together. Rather, he spent my time with his other kids. The ones he shared with his wife. I knew nothing specific about them but assumed he showed them love, attention, and protection, things he never showed me. Second, I was upset because he lived more securely than my mother and I did. He lived in Virginia Beach;

to me, that was like living in the Hamptons. We lived in a working-class neighborhood in Portsmouth and survived off my mother's retirement. He had a car, but we didn't. He had a job at the shipyard and retired from the Navy. My mom was disabled and couldn't work. He wore a nice suit whenever he came from work, and my mother struggled to keep basic clothing on my back. Third, and most importantly, I was heated because he didn't protect me. I endured abuse and wished he had been there to shield me from family and peer rejection and from being molested by a neighborhood pastor. If he had been there, maybe I would've been safe.

I hated him. I wanted him to save me from what was my life, and he didn't. I wanted him to give me peace, yet he added to my torment. At one point, if he had been starving on the street, I wouldn't have given him a slice of bread. Why should I care for him when he didn't care about me? We had no relationship. Just writing the word father in this chapter is uncomfortable because I never referred to him with such affinity. After all, he was never my father, dad, daddy, or any of those other cute names used to identify the male participant in my creation. I felt that Santiago never prioritize me in his life. I was an afterthought. On many occasions, he would choose others, silently relegating me to the background of his life. He made no appearances at school events, birthday parties, or major milestone events. Not even at my lowest moment, my mother's funeral. I was 18 and needed a parent, but I went without because he chose to ignore my anguish. He was a no-show, and I felt abandoned by both parents. I was hollow and an orphan with no one.

His absence was the hardest to accept, making me feel worthless. Not even the love I got from my mother and other family members could fill the void of his presence. I thought that since he didn't want me, no one would. I feared that I'd be alone for the rest of my life which negatively impacted my ability to trust others, especially men. I couldn't trust they would support or protect me because he didn't. My response was to make him and any man with whom I had a relationship love me on my terms. I became clingy and needy in any male relationship. My mindset was if they thought they could abandon me, they were wrong. Eventually, I sought Santiago's attention more frequently. I would call him requesting time for my children under the guise they needed to know their grandfather. But what I really wanted was for him to validate, accept and be proud of me. It worked until I needed more, and he could not deliver.

I also became insecure when my efforts for his attention failed. I doubted who I was as a human being and believed that his rejection must have been my fault. He would be happily married without issues if I wasn't born. He wouldn't have to make veiled attempts at pretending to care. I must be the bad element in this relationship, I thought. So, I focused on being the good aspect. He was part of the reason I became a perfectionist. I had to be perfect because my mother demanded it and because he would finally see me if I was perfect. But I also shrank and became reclusive to a point. I didn't build relationships because I was afraid of further rejection. I stayed home with my mom because she was my security. I doubted my outer looks. If I were prettier, he would surely accept me. He wouldn't be ashamed to claim me as his if I was taller with a better style. I had so many ifs and no real answers as to why our relationship, or lack thereof, was in such shambles. But I continued to hope that he would make it right.

Then, there was the day he completely pulverized any thought that I would ever be truly validated. I was sitting in the den at his house. I was about 38. By this time, I was welcomed into his home, and it was one of my regular visits, but on this occasion, I asked to do an interview of sorts with him. I had no regular involvement with him until I was 27, so I wanted to learn more about his life and mine. First, he told me about growing up in Puerto Rico and New York and life in the Navy. Next, he shared about his travels and offered clarification about his children, who lived in several locations across the globe. Finally, when we discussed myself, I asked, "Did you miss me not being in your life?"

"No," was his quick reply, "I had other children to occupy my time."

I followed with, "Do you have any regrets?"

"No. I would live my life the same if I had to do it all over again."

Then silence. "Okay." Was my only audible response.

I was hurting so bad from his confession, but I could not allow him to see me broken, so I hastily left. I soon realized what I felt was the result of tiny punctures administered over years of neglect by this man. I withered into a shell and eventually cut all contact with him. That sounds harsh, but God had been urging me to do so for some time, and I didn't listen because he was the man I knew as a dad. But God was insistent, "Let go and stop talking to him. Break the tie." But if I stopped talking to him, who would be my father?

This was when my life started to change.

For years, all I wanted was a piece of his heart, any piece that would make me feel loved. Pursuing pieces of him yielded fragments in me that would require a plan for healing and my letting go. I needed to grieve him, but he was alive and well, unlike my mother. However, the process was the same as grieving the dead. I went through all the stages: anger, depression, bargaining, denial, and finally, acceptance.

When the urge to contact him surfaced, I would ask God to help me understand why the separation was necessary and help facilitate a reconnection if it was the Lord's will. I knew God would strengthen me during these moments. I remained resolute, and as a result, I began to heal, but I never spoke to Santiago again. He died three years after our separation.

The heart of the matter is...

While writing this chapter, my editor, Monique, asked me to do homework. She said to ask God what's true about my relationship with my father and my life. When I asked God-heavy questions like that, I didn't know if I really expected him to provide me with heavy answers that undoubtedly stunned me.

First, I expected so much from Santiago. He needed to be present and active in my life and protect me from all harm. I wanted him to be a friend of sorts with whom I could share things, and I needed him to provide for my well-being. In all that, I never asked about God's expectations of him. When I did, I was shaken. God said, "Santiago, **Your Father**, was everything I expected him to be. He contributed the seed to bring you into this world and taught you lessons about your expectations for people. That was his role. Your problem is you don't think like me." Whew, Chile! I realized I was not God. I believe God's way is perfect. That means HE is perfect in all things, including God's expectations for the people in my life. I needed to stop thinking only about what I wanted from relationships and ask God about the purpose of that connection for me. Once I opened my heart to that, it released the beginning of accepting Santiago as my father. This couldn't work if my relationship with my Creator was not right.

But God wasn't done. I had to deal with my abandonment issues too. I catastrophized the abandonment by generalizing it with all my relationships. No one wanted me or loved me because he didn't. Not true. God showed me that my mother was a true ride-or-die soldier where I was concerned, and she was an awesome parent. She always told me I was beautiful and loved. She attended all my school performances, field trips, and parent-teacher conferences. She was a room mother and active member of the PTA until I graduated high school. I was always fed and clothed, even with her meager retirement, and when I wanted anything, 9 times out of 10, I got them. It may have taken her some time, but I did receive them. She listened to me; everyone knew I was her baby, especially when they jeopardized my safety and happiness. The only reason she didn't assault my abuser was that I never told her about the incidents for fear that she would go to jail for killing the bastard. I felt her love, honesty, protection, and even her crazy demands for me to be great. I never doubted who I was in her eyes. I was Mavis, aka

Granny, her baby, and I was treasured until she died. I still feel her love today.

Finally, God reminded me through Monique that grace is not earned. It's given freely. God prompted me to understand how important forgiveness is. It is a commandment. I want to stick it to those who have wronged me but want them to forgive me when I wrong them. How crazy is that? I think about all that I owe God....so much that I could never repay what it truly costs to wipe my slate clean. Yet, with a simple forgive me, it is done, and all is gone, never to be thought of or used against me again. Knowing this profound truth, how dare I not forgive my dad for the debt he owes me as his daughter? I must forgive, and as I write this sentence, I realize that finally, at long last, I have forgiven him. I feel light and free, and the anger is gone. Unknowingly, I even started talking about him in a positive light after I met with my editor. She was truly the blessing I needed to get free of hurt, rejection, anger, and unforgiveness. I am grateful, and I have peace.

From my healed heart to your hurting heart...

Give up your requirements for God's plan. Trust Him to orchestrate divine relationships. Don't be so rigid that you try to hold on to your preconceived notions about what is expected of the people in your life. Surrender that the Creator will protect your heart and spirit. Be slow in demanding people live up to your

47

expectations and allow God to control others' purposes in your life story. Learn to accept people for who they are and trust that God surrounds you with the right spirits to help push you to your destiny. At the end of the day, I never went without my father's love, and you aren't either. Santiago Rivera, aka my dad, loved me the best way he knew how, and it was part of God's plan from the beginning. All those nights I cried, wanting a daddy, God was there waiting for me to acknowledge my need for His love and the love of the people He placed in my life, like my mother. He's waiting for you to do the same. So release your expectations and latch on to God's love. It's worth it because you're worth it.

Fragments of a Young Girl's Heart

Charita Waddy

One hard stare is all it took for me to question my identity. Then, feeling like a pandora's box had been opened, I returned to that little child who always asked, "Where do I fit in?"

As a young girl growing up in inner-city projects with a household of three sisters, I often felt out of place. I wanted to be the baby, and at other times being older left me unsure. I was raised in a stern and structured yet abusive home. I saw my father abuse my mother. I was fondled by kinfolks. And the sternness I got from my grandma, all of it combined, made me feel invisible. I did not have the attention my sisters had from my mom. I didn't receive protection from my dad. Nor did I get the kind of affectionate love my younger sister got from my grandmother. These experiences left me with the nagging query, "what about me?" I recall having to put myself in a corner or closet hiding from the agony of hearing her cry or hoping not to be found so I wouldn't be touched. I was always crying and asking anybody for help, leaving me feeling alone, unloved,

49

unprotected, and confused. Longing to feel secure, I admired my sister's strength, outlook, and attitude. I wanted to be like them. From their clothing style to their choice of hair do's, I mirrored them. But I failed miserably as I wore big clothes, no named shoes, and because of my choice of friends, I was constantly teased. That eventually led me to build a wall of protection to defend myself from others.

Having a sassy mouth and bad attitude, along with now a shapely body, was just the beginning of the change in me. I adapted to my surroundings, which caused my mom to notice something different about me. She quickly moved us to a rural, suburban area (predominantly white) that voided my personal growth. Still, for her, it was putting us in a better place, or so she thought. Meeting new people and attending a new school made me question again: Where do I fit in? Struggling to make friends, I started doing things just to fit in, be accepted, and try to cover up the things that had happened to me. I lived a new lifestyle that was not accepted by many but worked for me. From middle to high school, I battled with how others would receive me, leading to more isolation. My walls became even higher and wider. Ultimately, I started doing and accepting anything that would allow me to be noticed. I needed to be an it girl. I went from dating a high school sweetheart to being with a drug dealer. He gave me things that allowed me to dress how I wanted and to wear my hair as I felt. I had the attitude that I didn't need anyone, and I moved to the beat of my drum. I slowly got to know more things about myself and who I was. I identified characteristics about myself that I used to build my own identity. I no longer walked in the shadow and image of my two sisters.

Shortly after taking on the love of hair and finding my style, the list of friends grew more and more, all while I was learning how to hold onto the ropes of life. Thinking I finally did something to be accepted by others and to fit in, my popularity took off until it was shattered by friends spreading rumors. What they said ranged from me being ugly, to gay, a whore, to not knowing how to do hair. I was crushed and reverted to a bubble of being to myself again and turning life off. I did not understand then that I had allowed people to have more validation of me than I had of myself. I was living a lifestyle that worked for them, not the real me. My life was spiraling. And I was close to death from dealing with an abusive guy just to uphold that image for others. Not knowing what to do, I ran – in the wrong direction. I stayed busy. I hung out, stealing, smoking, drinking, and perhaps even being a yes girl, but I didn't look back.

After high school, I became a mother and knew I had someone to love and accept me for who I was, no matter what I wore or looked like. I did everything I could to be a great mother to not just one but two

51

children. That feeling of unconditional acceptance from my kids had me on top of the world, and it didn't matter what others had to say. I allowed my everyday focus to be on my kids. It gave me a sense of feeling needed, wanted, and loved. Although it got overwhelming at times having two small children back-to-back, but I had purpose, passion, and a new way of looking at life.

Motherhood was my safe space. For so long, it took the weight off of me to figure out what was next. I was not a perfect mom by far, but I was determined not to have them feel as I once did. I pushed them to understand that having certain characteristics didn't make them. Still, it does help in honing in on their true identity. Now my children are adults, and my new role as a grandmother doesn't require as much, but that thing called identity has resurfaced. Not knowing which approach to take or direction to go, I find myself back at this familiar place of "what about me?" Realizing that I no longer want to settle for what characteristics previously defined me but accepting there's more to my life and a whole new identity of me. I'm learning new things about that scared little girl who didn't fully have a chance to live out her own life.

The heart of the matter is...

Everyone, including me, has had circumstances that have caused us to veer off from the people we aspire to be. Like Snow White, I will always have a mirror mirror on the wall experience that may resurface at any time, causing me to ponder my identity. Over time, I'm guilty of spreading myself thin by using other people's issues and running to their rescue to feel needed. I've overplayed my roles and titles as mother, daughter, sister, friend, significant other, and now grandmother to feel loved. For attention, I made sure I was dressed from head to toe and that I was seen. All of this has been a way to block me from my own issues and to deter me from the one necessary and most important thing...me.

I am determined to no longer be a prisoner by an identity created for everyone except me. I can honestly admit everything I could offer others was merely what I needed for myself, a voice, protection, security, acceptance, and unwavering love. Although I am unaware of what may still be in store for me, I feel compelled to release what no longer serves me and has taken precedence over my life. I was confused yet comfortable and complacent in areas when I truly wanted more. Not fully knowing if I'm scared to remove the fear due to failing or just reluctant to walk in my change. I know now; I have to do it. Understanding all the protection I thought I was giving myself was prolonging me from what lies ahead. Writing this is my first step towards a new me and beginning.

I'll admit to feeling a bit perplexed by this newfound outlook at this stage in life, but I do believe I am never too old to learn something new and try a different way. Changes are inevitable, but I have the capability to create my own change, and I'm going to grab hold of it and go for it.

From my healed heart to your hurting heart...

Suppressing was my way of sustaining myself until it was no more room left within. I have a mind filled with purpose and a heart filled with passion that will not be wasted due to a lack of effort. I'm striving ahead for my greater cause, and even if it seems unclear at this moment, I'm willing to give it all I got. I've envisioned the process, and it seems harder than it really is. Still, when I truly acknowledge what I held in for so long, it feels so good to finally let it out. Accepting that I cannot control how others view me or what they say, I'm exhaling from this part of my heart. I will no longer feel like I'm ashamed or embarrassed of myself or what others may think they know about me. Daily, I walk with my head high into my destiny. Building from the fragments of my broken heart, this is a series of first steps to creating and owning the new me. This is my story and the truth of finally finding my identity.

Fragments of a Vulnerable Heart

Tiffany M. Roberts

Letter to 14-year-old self

Hey little girl, stop while you can. You're only 14 years old; trust me, you don't know the cost of your next decision, and I'm not talking about the financial implications. Mental and emotional destruction are big ticket items you can't afford to pay. With the challenges of living in a low-income, high-crime area with many distractions, staying focused and submitting to the foundational expectations of a child your age isn't easy. Since you were eight years old, sadness has been building up slowly, but now this feeling is becoming overwhelming. Something seems to be missing, and your heart is yearning for fulfillment. One thing you know is the deep desire to hear and feel expressions of love from your father is troubling you. He is within arm's length in the stable home he established for your family but is mentally disjointed and seemingly emotionally preoccupied. He expresses love uniquely, ensuring his family never goes without the essentials in life. No matter what you do, he doesn't seem to notice you craving his intimacy and validation, and you have no clue how to express this need to him. Feeling deprived because you observe his ability to show happiness with people outside of your home fuels your curiosity, which builds into anger because you wish that version of him could be your experience. Yes. The good times you share with him, like traveling to National Parks, various states, beautiful beaches, and even local venues, are refreshing and keep you hopeful for future possibilities. Then there are the times when he degrades you by using debilitating words to describe you, referring to you as stupid and dumb, and even saying you would never be anything, which pulls you backward. Never understanding why he says these horrible things, out of the respect that he demands, you are forbidden to ask. Despite this, you still believe he is a great person and father who loves hard, just differently. Negative words and lack of affection are your kryptonite, the weapon of mass destruction. The darkness of low self-esteem and self-worth is taking root within you, and now you hate what you see in the mirror. The degree of resentment and outrage you build in silence is enigmatic.

High school years are becoming dreadful. While your academic performance was once meaningful to you, it quickly dwindles as you mentally drift. Stewarding valuable friendships is descending because you have directed your attention toward a man who is 22 years old, and remember you are only 14, and that eight-year age gap is far too advanced for you. He is seemingly subtly pursuing you, and your feelings are intensifying as his eloquent words, sensual touches, and intimate acts toward you have you physically and emotionally captivated. Making solid decisions is not your strong suit, and it would be in your best interest to end this before your vulnerability is violated. The void you are trying to fill will become anguish and regret in the coming years. Family relationships are becoming strained, especially with your father, as your rebellious behavior gradually becomes bolder. Many people are urging you to end this unhealthy relationship for obvious reasons. Over time you notice his appetite for multiple young girls; however, you have not been able to validate his actions with them. It isn't long before his entanglements are no longer secrets. Long story short, you just learned he had sex with you and two of your teenage friends on the same day and in the same bed. The feeling of disgust and what you imagine being treated like a filthy whore on the streets is crushing. Preying on your naivety, he convinces you that you are his main girl while completely belittling the others, and you foolishly decide to stay with him. At the expense of your high school experience, you do everything you can to maintain this toxic relationship. Guess what happens next? Tiffany, you are failing your 12th-grade English class, and your teacher just informed you are not eligible to graduate. Desperation kicks in, and you express to her your willingness to do anything to change this outcome. Unfortunately, it is too late. Your embarrassment and shame are indescribable as you fail and cannot graduate with your class peers. You have lived up to your father's negative perspective of you. Although humiliated, you passed the class during the summer, but quietly with no celebration.

The magnitude of your poor connection choice is finally starting to take a toll on you, but you are in so deep it seems impossible to walk away. A ridiculous amount of drama surfaced, but you stay because you have nowhere to go. It has become intolerable for your parents to allow you to continue to stay out all night and undermine their rules, and eventually, during a brutal confrontation, your father kicks you out of the house. This forces you to stay with your boyfriend, who lives with his mother. One day you start reflecting on all your boyfriend's lying, cheating, and manipulation, and you fume angrily. Finally, you decide to stand up for yourself; you make it clear to him that you want out. Unfortunately, the complexity of making this declaration was far from simple, and what happens next will almost cost you your life.

What would be a normal night together ends as a night of terror. You hear this inaudible scream in your head as you enter his room, with a sense of intense energy, but nothing too abnormal for your relationship. Then you are sitting on the edge of the bed, full of anxiety, but only seconds pass until matters quickly escalate, not realizing you will be held hostage for hours. Forced to put headphones over your ears, you hear his pre-recorded message saying, "If you ever leave or cheat on me, I will kill you." The deafening silence appears again, but this time you only hear the extremity of your heart pounding through your ears. In utter disbelief, you jump up to leave but enraged; he demands you to sit down. Moments later, you are staring at a black, heavy, long-barreled, dusty rifle aimed toward your stomach. As ignorant as you are about guns, you know that if he pulls the trigger at close range, it will blow your little body into pieces. With endless tears running down your face and pleading for your life, you desperately attempt to convince him you will fully commit to him to end this torture. Hours later, you are exhausted and finally scream, "Just pull the trigger." Flashbacks are taking place in your mind of all the terrible things that have happened, and you blame yourself for all of it. Feeling unworthy of being alive, loved, cared for, and saved, you believe you are better off dead. His whole posture shifts, and suddenly he is pleading for your forgiveness and the secrecy of this incident. He finally puts the gun down while also unlocking the door. Completely dehydrated, you dash out of the room to his mother, who is sound asleep downstairs. She is so oblivious and devastated at that moment that she protects you by putting you in her room. You think she may involve law enforcement or at least direct you to them, but she mentions nothing. You don't blame her for protecting her son, but you question why she will not do more for you. There you are, laying in her bed, crying all night with no consolation. At this moment, you become accustomed to dealing with trauma alone and in silence to the point where your deepest cries for help cannot even be projected audibly. No one sees nor shields you from the pain invading your life. You are now programmed not to ask for help. Somehow you are accepting that life is supposed to be this way. By the way, you will not build up the strength or courage to leave the relationship for another three years; when you do, it will come with many obstacles. I'm proud of you because you will work hard to become the lady you will be.

Transformative Perspective

In my mid to late 20s, the pain from my experiences was excruciating, and I felt as if my soul had been scorched. At that point, I knew my heart was operating on fumes, and needed to protect it. I built the strength to shift my focus from wanting someone to love me to make notable achievements. On paper, I struck out every negative word spoken and action taken against me. I graduated from college magna cum laude, held prestigious positions in Corporate America, transformed my 325-credit score and became a single homeowner while raising an amazing son, and so much more. My brokenness still haunted me through all these successes, and the reality of my past trauma continued to resurface. Many hurtful words were spoken, but I couldn't shut off the ones my dad said to me. My heart had been broken so much that I thought it irreparable. I developed triggers that were easily set off anytime I perceived a risk posed to my safety by others. The excuse I used to justify my behavior was constantly affirming I had trust issues. This mindset carried into some of my adult relationships and shaped my behavior. I deliberately chose to be involved where no strings attached because it seemed easier than the risk of someone further bruising my heart. In one relationship, I became physically abusive toward a man. I know it was because I spent all those years prior not standing up for myself, so it didn't matter if his intentions were harmful or not; I was protecting myself at all costs. My thinking was so warped that I blamed him for my actions for triggering me. Despite my toxic actions, he was patient, and I fell in love with him. He made it clear upfront that he had no intentions of leaving his relationship, but the intimacy we shared gripped my heart unexpectedly. Eventually, I felt used by him and angry at myself for allowing him to treat me this way. Retrospectively, it became clear he catered to and nurtured the void I longed for from my childhood. I could no longer allow my heart to bleed, so I ended the relationship.

This is where my real inward healing started. I became severely depressed and plotted ways to end my life. I experienced agony as if I was shut up in the room being held at gunpoint all over again. My cries for help were silent and completely undetected by everyone. My outward and perceived inward appearance rendered many compliments but baffled me because no one knew my true condition. After all, I had been through; I despised myself for the decisions I made and the people who participated in them. On top of that, I was ashamed to admit my life was such a mess while serving in ministries and supporting others at my church. I distinctly remember sitting in that church one Sunday, and the pastor preached a powerful message titled "Setbacks are Setups for Blessings." I wept internally as it seemed my eyes could not produce tears. Still, inside, it felt like an atomic bomb was ready to explode. At that moment, I knew I had to go back and pick up all the fragments of myself that I had given away and lost along the way.

When I started mental health therapy, my guard was high, and I had difficulty acknowledging I had been verbally, emotionally, physically, and sexually abused. Oddly, I had grown accustomed to accepting blame for every circumstance and wanted to protect my offenders. My pride, lack of trust, and embarrassment were more important to me than my healing, which stifled my therapist's ability to help me. Eventually, my guard came down, and digging up the roots of my trauma helped me recognize the correlation between the lack of emotional intimacy with my father and my poor choices in different areas of my life. I wanted my father's validation, wisdom, love, and protection. I do not fully understand why I was left with this hole in my heart, but I do understand true unconditional love and forgiveness, which allowed me to make peace with it all. Unfortunately, I learned that he was incapable of doing love my way. Based on his behavior, I believe he channeled life through his experiences and places of pain I did not know. I could not begin to imagine what he must have been experiencing inside, let alone what his past was like if his outputs were as such.

The heart of the matter is...

While some of the things my father said to me were foul and damaging, I realized that I had to see him from his angle versus my own, and through that, I could forgive him and love him for who he was versus who I created him to be in my mind. This didn't excuse his behavior, but it freed me from the offense I held against him and helped me to see him through a selfless lens. I hated him for many reasons when I was in my 20s, and as contradictory as these emotions sound, I wanted to love him at the same time. I forgave him so my actions could foster the love I desired from him. I wholeheartedly believe he did the best he could based on his life experiences. He simply expressed his love by being an amazing provider. I am 48 years old, and have no memory of even hugging him in my life. The first time I heard my father tell me he loved me was on his deathbed in 2020. It was not the magical moment I had imagined because I had already shifted my love posture toward him in my 30s and was able to receive his love the way he could provide it. I was already at peace. I I have no memory of even hugging him in my life. I am thankful I didn't live the rest of his life with resentment and regret.

From my healed heart to your hurting heart...

As a result of what I lacked in my dad, my heart became vulnerable to a man I perceived as a father figure but retrospectively had predatory tendencies. I didn't realize how hard I condemned myself for my decisions over the years when God had already forgiven me. Finally, I came to terms with the fact that at age 14, I was oblivious to my decision and what would happen to me. My self-esteem and self-worth seemed damaged beyond repair, but once I forgave myself, started to love who I was, and understood my value, my transformation took place in this area too.

I could truly be internally what people observed me to be externally. I realized that as I became stronger, my discernment sharpened, my weaknesses became harder to detect, and I attracted a different caliber of people. Erasing the toxicity of love was required to see me and others differently. My healing journey took time, sacrifice, and patience. However, I know my trauma made me who I am today, and I am able to stand in my truth, no longer ashamed of any part of my experience. In fact, through this process of sharing, I discovered my voice for the very first time. I am a happily married woman who learned to love and be loved the right way by an amazing man.

Fragments of a Waiting Heart

Marcia L. Ali

It was a cool autumn afternoon in September. I was strolling down Broad Street in downtown Newark New Jersey. No biggie, 'cause I was just out doing what I always did. Shopping for something cute to wear. My favorite spot was High Voltage, a famous boutique back in the day. As the breeze and the sun rays highlighted my face, I stopped at the crosswalk of Broad and Market and waited for the light to change. Green means go, so I went, and standing at the bus stop was him. I felt a slight thrill deep in my soul. Okay, let me keep it all the way real. My heart fluttered. It was Yancy. Well, at least that was his name when we were growing up. He had changed his name to Ali. He was a bad boy and four years older than me. He was one of those ones that I was supposed to stay away from. I said to myself maybe he's different now. Anyway, we locked eyes, and I tried to act like I didn't see him. He yelled my name. Marcia...Marcia Gibson. I stopped and stared at this well-built, brown-eyed, chocolate, wavy-haired man. He had on a full-length black leather coat and a silk shirt with just enough buttons left open to make that chest pop. His pants were bright in color, and his shoes were fire, black with strips of lizard. The boy could always dress. Sheesh. I hadn't got close enough to him before to see all this goodness, but that day I came face to face with the one I soon thought would rescue me from life and bring me so much joy. From that encounter on the corner of Broad and Market, we exchanged numbers and became the best of friends. We had beepers back then, so whenever I got that little buzz with our special code, I felt like I was on top of the world. We talked every single day. They were the kind of conversations in that we said nothing. I was just happy to be on the phone with the one who stole my heart. Those wee hours of the morning when we asked are you sleep and both of us lied and said, "no, I'm just thinking." Lol. This went on for months. We were not sexually intimate, so I was sure this one would be different. I felt he respected me on a different level.

Eventually, we met each other's families. Well, I kind of knew his family already. With Ali being popular in town, he knew of mine. My dad was top brass in the police department, so surely nobody wanted to meet him. Shoot, after my first husband, I told myself, I know my dad will be like, what is her damn problem? So, I slowly walked that introduction, but they later became like father and son. Ali wined and dined me. We shopped, and he always made sure we looked good. From top-of-line shoes to tailored-made suits. Our favorite restaurant was on Route 22, called the Ground Round. It was a steakhouse that had peanut shells on the floor. This went on for several months. I was just talking, laughing, hanging out, and cooking for him; I am a good cook, and he loved my cooking. In April, I became known as Ali's girl. He taught me independence and helped me to reach for more. I was on public assistance, and he thought that was trifling. I went to school, became a Pharmacy Tech, and got two jobs. In October, Ali, I, and two of our sons were in a horrific car accident. Instantly my life changed. Through a cloud of smoke, I heard sirens, equipment, and people talking and crying. The entire car dashboard was wrapped around me. Glass was everywhere. As I peeked out the driver's side window, I heard an unfamiliar voice say, "She's not dead. Her chest is moving." Then, I heard the loud screeching sounds from the Jaws of Life cutting the door open to remove me from the vehicle. I was in the hospital for twenty-seven days. Ali became my knight in shining armor. He took care of everything that concerned me, including my son. I was so impressed with him taking care of business like any good man would. We were back like nothing had ever happened when I was released from the hospital. Going on dates and doing family outings. Ali had a big old Lincoln Towne car. It was deep burgundy with a half-rag vinyl top with white wall tires. Oh, how we rode that car. I remember when he let me drive that big beauty in the snow. I came home from work with three flat tires. He was hot as fish grease. It was a long time before I drove his car again. Soon after, he bought me my own car. I was moving on up like Weezie from the Jeffersons.

Around year two of courting, I baked him a cake and wrote on it, "Will you marry me?" He never answered, but he followed suit. We looked at rings galore. I tried to be modest because I didn't want to seem like a gold digger. Even still, I looked at rings that I felt he couldn't afford. I told him whatever he picked would be fine with me. I eyed one ring that had a marquis cut center stone surrounded by baguette diamonds. I had already resolved that I wasn't getting that ring, but it was bad. The day he picked my ring up, I let my mouth get the best of me, jumped out of the car, and walked home. I didn't even know he had bought the ring. I thought he couldn't afford it. I bet he thought I was crazy. Finally, we had the bomb engagement party. He rented out a club in Irvington, New Jersey, and the whole town was invited. We set a date for our wedding, but soon our plans were intercepted by a family tragedy. This took a toll on Ali financially, and in the midst of my excitement, I knew this meant I had to wait. Although I understood, I hated waiting. After all, I had already waited six years. Frustrated but excited, we continued planning our big day. Little did I know we would have the wedding that would be the talk of the town for years to come. People are still talking about our wedding today. A wedding fit for a Queen. He paid for whatever I wanted. We had a sit-down plated dinner in one of the finest dining experience establishments in New Jersey, the Pantagis Restaurant. We gathered with two-hundred guests on March 28, 1997, and said our I do's. We danced the night away. I felt like I was on top of the moon, and all my troubles would soon be over. On our wedding night, amongst the good-good loving, we laughed and talked about how we had finally made it to being husband and wife.

As trouble always found its way, my now husband was injured, and we decided to relocate. Reluctantly I moved, leaving everything and everyone I knew behind. That was hard. I was a Newark girl. I had finally found a good job, and now we were moving. I dragged my feet because I knew I had obstacles to overcome. The biggest one was passing a drug screen to get a job. I was getting high and knew I was about to be exposed. I had told my husband I had stopped, but it wasn't true. Eventually, I got sober and found a good job in Virginia. A few years later, there was a layoff, but I was blessed with the opportunity to go to nursing school. So here we were in a new state, and I had to start again. Ali was an entrepreneur and still had his store in New Jersey. His business forced him to commute once a month. This was cool at first, but after a while, it caused strain on our marriage. I felt neglected and rejected. He paid the bills, but I wanted more; I wanted him. This was the cycle of our first ten years of marriage. Neither of us had a grounded example of a good marriage. We were both products of divorced parents. To him, stuff meant love, and I needed time and affection. In spite of building a home in a new development, there was still something missing between us. We had constant conflict as we grew further apart over the years. I made some choices that were not healthy for me or my marriage. The house, the cars, and the gifts no longer meant anything to me. We did counseling for a while, but that only lasted for a moment. It seemed like things never went back to the way it was. Sure, we had periods of great times, but then there was the spiraling of disagreements and disappointments that overshadowed the good.

I was later diagnosed with Multiple Sclerosis, which added to the list of delays in my life. Amid my health crisis, my best friend and mom-in-love were diagnosed with cancer. I took on being their caregiver but forgot about caring for myself. I had become a nurse and felt I could handle it along with my personal life. Yet, here I was, faced with another delay. To me, this was another disappointment and failure. My heart was hurting from constant frustration. The death of my best friend, losing my nom-in-love, personal failures, and my marriage were all weights that I knew delay would again be a part of my process.

The heart of the matter is...

I began counseling because I was always feeling down. I was diagnosed with clinical depression. Then, I realized that my expectations of others came from a wounded heart. Through the Word of God, I knew I could choose to speak life or death, but I wasn't prepared to eat the fruit of my past words. All the days, I said, "he makes me sick. I wish he would go away." I gave up my God-given authority and accepted defeat instead of victory. I forfeited my strength for weakness. I sat in doubt instead of trusting God completely with everything that concerned me. I said some really mean things to my husband, all in the name of defending myself. I often apologized; however, my words had taken root and grew. Trust me when I say there is no peace in disobedience. I allowed the enemy to muzzle my prayer life. I had to repent for waiting with the wrong posture. Some days I forgot I was a believer. I forgot I belonged to Jesus. My pain was real, yet I chose comfort instead of peace. My emotions were inconsistent, so I had to learn to guard my mouth (I am still working on this) and let God protect my heart. Proverbs 4:23 (KJV) Keep thy heart with all diligence; for out of it are the issues of life. I had to constantly declare what God says, not my feelings or circumstances. I now know my feelings are fickle and are not facts. I never really sat with God and asked him if I was in his will with my marriage or anything else for that matter. I was conditioned to pray during and after the chaos had happened. Life changed as our kids grew up, and our grandchildren became our new focus. We were rescue rangers for everyone else except us. Constantly buried in work and day-to-day tasks. I soon recognized that I didn't even know what I liked anymore for me. We grew further and further apart. Simple discussions quickly escalated into bickering and arguments. The trust was gone, and my hope for us was on life support. Conversations turned from working it out to getting out.

As I sit in a separated state from Ali, it hurts like hell. I've given thirty-two years of myself to one phase of life. I thought I was living, but now I know I simply have been existing. With tears flowing as I write this, I understand that I am the one who is responsible for my happiness, not my husband. He was to compliment the gift I brought to the marriage, not complete it. I was a broken, wounded little girl who felt abandoned, and my husband couldn't heal that for me.

Waiting on God is hard. I struggle with waiting because I've always been the fixer. If there was nothing to fix, I felt unproductive. I simply wanted to live my best life, yet I had to grasp that I didn't even know what my best life was or could be. This alone had taken so much time from me when all I had to do was go to the one who had all the answers. That one was and still is God. So now, with therapy, I am still peeling through the layers of my healing. I am still waiting on God because he loves me enough to wait on me. I am enough. As a matter of fact, I am more than enough.

Lastly, I did not take the time to heal enough to be whole. My heart posture was wrong. I had to repent for being so far out of God's will for my life. I learned that peace and comfort are two different things, and I had to make up my mind about which one I really wanted. Comfort had always been my feeling of choice. I wasn't robbed of my peace. I gave it away. My peace was often forfeited simply because I didn't have the courage to just wait on God. My enthusiasm was gone. I no longer asked God to speak to me because I was simply tired of waiting. The weight of waiting was too heavy for me to carry alone. Then the revelatory moment of sitting with my editor came while discussing my writing for this anthology. The Lord clearly said to me, "You didn't wait; You quit." I was too done.

From my healed heart to your hurting heart...

Waiting requires us to have the correct posture with God. We are required to be yielded to His Word. Our ears have to be open to hear his voice. According to

James 2:26, "For as the body without the spirit is dead, so faith without works is dead also." I finally let go of control, and now I give God permission to have his way. God goes not, nor has he ever needed my help.

There is an old hymn titled "On Christ The Solid Rock I Stand" written by Edward Mote. It says, "

I dare not trust the sweetest frame but wholly lean on Jesus' name.

On Christ, the solid rock, I stand; all other ground is sinking sand."

This Marcia - has surrendered it all. I have yielded every piece of my life to Christ. What does that mean? It means I wait. It means I fight. If broken crayons can still color, surely the pieces of my shattered heart still have a purpose, and I know my wait will be worth it.

Fragments of a Disappointed Heart

Gwendolyn Winston-Marrow

I was eight years old the first time I met my father. He had come to Virginia for his family's annual reunion. I was excited and nervous at the same time. I had always wondered who he was and what he looked like. My mother told me he had moved to Pennsylvania with his parents before I was born. The next time I saw him, I was sixteen years old; it was the end of the school year, and I was in Philadelphia visiting my aunt, and he came to see me. Once again, he said how happy he was to see me and how sorry he was that he hadn't kept in touch. I said nothing, yet all the while, I was thinking liar, liar, tongue on fire. He stated he was married, had two sons, and took me to meet my brothers at this place called Willow Grove. It was really nice, and we had a lot of fun. I was glad that I had gotten to meet them. I felt like a part of his family for the first time. He asked me when I was leaving to return home, and I told him; he said, "Okay, I'll come to see you before you leave." He hugged me and left. When I returned home, my mother had moved out of my grandparent's house along with my two younger sisters and gotten her own apartment. I stayed with my grandparents.

I didn't see him again until he returned to Virginia for his family reunion. When he came, I let him know that I wanted him to do something for me. I said, "I want you to go with me to the Bureau of Vital Statistics and put your name on my birth certificate because my birth certificate shows Father – Unknown." He said, "No, I'm not doing that. I know you're my daughter, and you know I'm your father; you don't need no piece of paper to tell you that." I stood there biting my tongue and holding back the tears. I was so hurt, so disappointed; my heart ached. I could see he was upset too. He got in his car and promised to see me again, but that didn't happen. I felt like I had really messed up. After that, I didn't see him too often. When I did, I was reminded of our conversation about the birth certificate, and the pain of that disappointment would start all over again. I tried to forgive him and move on, but facing what I took as a rejection of myself was hard. I'm sure he thought it was no big deal, but what I heard was, "You are my daughter, but you just aren't good enough to carry my name."

Both of my brothers passed. The youngest drowned in a pool, and the older one died a few years later from alcohol poisoning. His death was difficult because we always talked about when I would see them again. I went to Philadelphia for their funerals but didn't spend much time with my dad. After that, I didn't see much of him, even though he still came to Virginia each summer for his family reunions. My mother saw him, but I did not. So, what was I supposed to do with all the disappointments, the emotional pain of rejection, and feelings of abandonment? Is this what the love of a father looks like? Could he only father a child in his house?

I spent my whole life looking for my father's love.

I was an elder at my church. I worked as a director for a daycare, bookkeeper, and secretary along with anything else asked, still working on getting the validation and approval I needed so badly. One Saturday morning at our 6:00 am intercessory prayer meeting, one of the ladies came to me and told me that rumors were going around in church that I was having an affair with the pastor and that I had stolen money from the church. I just stood there in shock. I couldn't believe it until that Monday; I got a phone call from the pastor's wife saying they needed to meet with me. In the pastor's office, the wife asked if I had heard the rumors about her husband and me, and I said, "yes, but I know it wasn't true, so I ignored it, but what I am really shocked about is the fact that you believe it." I was then advised I would not have any meetings or conversations with the pastor unless someone were present. Well, now I can't talk to my spiritual father. The next week I requested a meeting with them regarding the money I had been accused of stealing. I spoke with the bank, and it was discovered that the deacons had used the wrong deposit slip and put that week's deposit in the wrong account. The branch manager was going to transfer the money to the correct account. I asked if they had any other questions. Nothing was said, and I went back to work. I was so ready to leave, but I had to stay and endure the gossip, looks, and rolling eyes from the people who had called themselves my friends and even the pastor's children and family members.

I cried for days, attempting to do my job and walk with my head up. The people I thought were my friends were tearing down my character and questioning my integrity. It was over five months before I was finally released to leave. As I was given the mic from my spiritual father and pastor to say goodbye to the church I had been faithful to for over ten years, I was told that if I said anything inappropriate, I would be asked to sit down, and the microphone would be taken from me. I took the mic, thanked everyone for all they had done for my family and me, and said I would never forget them and continue praying for them. It was one of the best and worst days of my life. It's amazing the things I had to endure because I was still looking for validation, and all I got was more disappointment.

The heart of the matter is...

All of this happened to me because I was still seeking approval and validation from people. After all, I didn't get it from my father, family, or church members. I came to realize that I had set myself up for disappointment.

1. My mother was fifteen when she got pregnant and was sixteen when I was born. My father was nineteen, and when my mother was two months pregnant, he left town and moved to Philadelphia with his parents. Even though my grandparents were there for my mother, I know she must have felt abandoned by him. Neither one of my parents knew anything about being a parent. They were babies having babies. I put expectations on them that neither of them could meet. As a child, I didn't understand or know why things were happening or not happening for me. I just wanted my parents to be there for me like my friend's parents at school and in the neighborhood were for them. Maybe I shouldn't have had to carry the weight of it all, but I did. Life didn't always work out how I wanted, but I kept moving forward. Yes, the disappointments were real, and they may have been justified. However, it still wasn't fair for me to hold my heart hostage to the failed

expectations I had placed on my parents, who couldn't give me what I felt I needed from them then. As an adult, I better understand the why, and I'm always working to restore that piece of my heart. Understanding the why helps the process, so ask yourself the necessary questions. Find the why, even if you can't allow it to be a teachable moment.

2. I spent years working and giving and doing to get the approval of others. When I checked the dictionary for the definition of approval, I found this: the belief that someone or something is good or acceptable. I used gifts, money, talents, and my time, whatever it took to make others happy because I wanted and needed their consent that badly. Continuing down that road only led me to anger, frustration, and disappointment when I didn't get the acceptance I thought it would bring. I accused people of using me, but I was the one who made myself available to them. I was the one who didn't say no. I had to forgive them for using me and myself for settling for whatever little attention I got when I was worth so much more. The forgiveness was for me so I could be free because unforgiveness had become very destructive. It ate away at my peace of mind, joy, character, and relationships. It is a cross that I chose not to

81

bear because it kept me in bondage for so long. At the same time, the offender(s) walked away, either unaware or just not caring how I felt or what I was going through. Forgive those who have hurt you, but most of all, forgive yourself daily.

3. I needed validation, especially from the people closest to me. It is recognition or affirmation that a person's feelings or opinions are valid or worthwhile. I allowed people to take advantage of me because I was afraid that if I didn't, they would leave me or not like me, and guess what? A lot of them did, anyway. I had to come to a place where no was the real and right response for me. Was I hurt and disappointed when they walked out of my life? Yes, but I understood they were not there for me but for what they could get from me. I had to find myself worthy. I must look at myself differently and change what needs to be changed in me and my mindset. My validation was no one's responsibility; it was and still is all mine. I am accepted in the beloved, and oh, what a wonderful thing it is. That validation will never change, and for that, I am grateful.

4. Because I reacted to things from an emotional place, disappointment was often the result.

Instead, I should have paused, taken a deep breath, thought about what happened, and asked, Why, and what was my role in it all? What was I to get from the experience? Was it that bad, or was I just angry because it wasn't done my way? Was it my pride that was hurt? There is more than one side (my side) to a situation. Sometimes, if I had stepped back and considered that, it might have eliminated some of the aching I experienced.

5. Instead of getting up and doing something about my issues, I wallowed in my self-centeredness and isolated myself. I just existed from one day to the next, not praying, not reading the Word, or doing anything that would help me. I watched television and played games on my cell phone. That was my way of escape. I had nothing positive to say to myself. I purchased books I knew would help and then did not read them. I was just waiting for the morning to come so I would not wake up. I felt I had no purpose left and was too old, and it was just too late for me. Self-sabotage had become my way of life. I was consistently just setting myself up for disappointment. I had to change what I spoke to and about myself and believe it! I could not receive that from anyone else until I began to love and believe in myself. So I began the

work, moment by moment, day by day. I spoke life to myself. What a painful but beautiful journey this has been, and the joy of it all is that it's not over, and I'm glad about it.

From my healed heart to your hurting heart:

Piece by piece, I still find parts of my heart that need to be worked on and healed. My heart is enjoying the good, bad, and ugly process. There is no magic formula that will make everything okay. It is hard and continuous work, but it is so worth it; you are so worth it.

I know you feel that the pain will never end but trust me, it is only temporary. We determine how long the temporary will be. The memory of the situation may not go away, but the actual pain of it will. We must do our best to keep our emotions in check; learn to respond and not react. We have to control our emotions and not allow our emotions to control us. Take a deep breath and hold on to your peace. We must have someone to talk to who will be a true confidant. Someone who will speak the truth and not only say what we want to hear. Go to a therapist if you need to, and know it is all right. Allow ourselves to grieve and to be happy at the same time.

I didn't have a true understanding of unconditional love. I thought that performance was connected to it. I considered being and doing what others needed me to be and do to be love. I have realized that I am loved even if I do nothing, and I remind myself of that daily. Now I do what I do because I'm loved and not to get love. There is a nugget that God gave me many years ago, "Look at what you can't see until you can't see what you're looking at." In other words, hold on to the dream and vision that God has given you and see that until you no longer see the pain, dysfunction, and disappointment that is currently around you. Change your focus; there is a future and hope.

Fragments of a Black Sheep's Heart

Cheron Johnson

I was sixteen when I woke up in a room trying to identify my surroundings, attempting to move and wiggle freely but to no avail. I was laid flat on my back, shackled to a hospital bed with restraints on my ankles and wrists. All types of machines were beeping and buzzing hooked up to me. Doctors and nurses came in and out, whispering amongst themselves. I lay looking for familiar faces, listening for voices, but I came up with no one. I was just stuck there. Then, as heavy tears overflowed my eye ducts, I watched my mother walk towards the bed. At that moment, I realized I had failed at my task of committing suicide. My last words to her hit me hard, "I took Grandma's medicine." That morning my mind was made up. I had given up, and each swallow of her pills confirmed that I had officially thrown the towel in. I didn't care what or who I hurt, and that included myself.

Before sixteen, I was never the child with a white picket fence, a family dog, or a two-parent household. I didn't see my parents together ever, let alone be cordial for the sake of me. The constant verbal altercations between them and what I witnessed weighed heavy on me. I would have never imagined that I would be eating breakfast before school, and one of my parents would slam their fists through the glass table because they were pissed off at the other. That was my reality.

My mother was much older than my father when I was conceived, so I was raised in a single-parent home with my mom. In my father's home, I was part of a blended family that began when I was five. Through the years, I pleaded to move in with him to be a part of his lifestyle. I wanted the life my siblings had - a family with two parents raising their children under one roof. I always felt like I was losing out because I was the outsider looking in. When I visited and then had to leave, I thought I had lost space in my dad's life more and more. At times months passed before I visited again on weekends because he had to work, he was busy, or I couldn't see him for other reasons. Although he spent money on me, that's not what my heart desired. It was simple, I wanted my dad. I yearned for the dad that my siblings had every day. When they were attending daddy-daughter dances, I wished for just one dance with him, to say the least. He was the superhero to them that I wanted for myself.

The day finally came when my request was answered. I was able to move in with him and his family. In the beginning, I was excited. I was a part of the type of household I described earlier, but that feeling didn't last long. I felt sorrow because I did not have an outlet to express myself or my feelings. The majority of the time, day-to-day life took priority. I stayed in my room with the door shut or worked my job just so I wouldn't have to be there. Regardless of being under the same roof, the disconnect was still noticeable. There were times I shut down with depression. I was struggling to be a fixture in the family because I was the foreigner coming into their world in reality. I started to detach myself emotionally. I showed little effort to take part. Of course, we went on family trips and outings, but my facial expressions were very modest. I didn't want to be there, and my conversations reflected it. My father constantly reminded me and compared me to an older cousin on how I should carry myself or be a better older sister with joy and excitement, as she exemplified. He chiseled away at my self-esteem whenever he compared me to someone else. My confidence felt inadequate as his daughter. In my eyes, he wanted me to be more of something or someone that I was not. It wasn't by coincidence that I started asking and questioning my identity. I would be lying if I didn't say his words and actions did not hurt. Because I couldn't be someone other than the individual I was, I began asking others what I could do differently to gain his approval. Instead of other high schoolers focused on growing and getting ready for college, I was focused on a level of admiration from my daddy.

I started to digress internally and was rebellious. Things at home had become more complicated. I was in and out of family court. My emotions and the animosity I felt were draining. I was caught between my parents and their annoyance for one another, and it was a bit challenging for me to handle. I loved my mother, but again, I desperately wanted to live with my father. In hindsight, he was overwhelmed and would take his frustration out on me. On our way to court one day, he was so upset he blurted out, "I hate you because you look like your mother, and if you were living with her, I wouldn't have to deal with this shit." I was in shock at the way he conveyed his feelings. I slid down in my seat because I felt so small, like I was a burden to him. Ideally, it wasn't the feeling I ever wanted to place in his heart for me. I thought I had strained his marriage by begging him to live in his home, which complicated things. My emotions were conflicted because of my family dynamics. I was jealous that my siblings were getting more of what I didn't have, which was the daddy-daughter relationship. I was also resentful due to his actions and verbiage towards me. Then we relocated to a new neighborhood, so I had to get accustomed to new friends and a new school, which was another hurdle I had to face. However, this new territory allotted me a little more freedom. I was working, and I met some school friends, so I hung out with them on a day-to-day basis. I would stay around their families just so I wouldn't have to be alone or put a Band-Aid on what I felt - angered pain.

The weekend of my Junior prom, I was on punishment and couldn't attend per my father's rules. Well, my mother knew of the prom and said I could go from her house because my father had no control over there. Of course, I was all for it. This particular weekend was Mother's Day, so I hung out with my family until it was time for my mother to take me home. I went into the house to grab some things. While looking out of the window, I saw an altercation on the front lawn. The next thing I knew, I was sandwiched between the adults, yelling and crying at them to stop fighting. I told my mom to leave, but my strength was nothing compared to theirs. The tension was so thick after that that nobody spoke for days. My father finally broke his silence after day two, but he was pissed, yelling, and full of fury. He said, "How could you bring your ghetto ass family to my home to traumatize my kids?" as if I wasn't one of his children. I was the one traumatized! One of my classmate's moms was nice enough to let me stay with them for a few weeks to finish school and let the air clear back at the house. But I never went back to live with my dad.

It was too much for him, the family, and me. I moved in with my grandmother. However, I had mental and emotional breakdowns throughout my stay with her. I was officially over any type of emotions that I felt; I had become numb. On a Sunday morning, my grandmother was taking me back to live with my mom, and Donnie McClurkin's song, "We Fall Down," was on the radio. I spoke to myself and said, I'm tired of feeling like a failure, incompetent and unintelligent. So, I took my grandmother's pills that were on her dresser. I thought there would be no more pain, and fighting between my parents, if I were no longer here. My suicide was happening. Shortly after I reached my mother's house, I was on the couch, and we were talking, but my words were slurred, and the medication had started doing its own thing. I heard her scream for help before I faded away.

Later on, in my adult years, I encountered more isolation. Instead of lying in a hospital bed, I was in a federal jail cell for over four years. Then, finally, I had nothing but time and God to run to.

The Truth of The Matter is obvious. I didn't know how to live life without acceptance.

1st Truth: I was wrong and a coward for attempting to take my own life. God is the giver of life. He gives and takes away (Job 1:21). He is the only one who decides when and how I should die. I allowed the enemy to enter my head and made

91

me think things would be much greater without me. As a result, I let him down, as well as myself. I have learned that no matter how tough it may seem, the word of God strengthens me in my darkest hours. When I feel weak, I must learn to get out of His way and let God's will do the work He promised.

2nd Truth: I was angry with God that I didn't have the traditional family setup. I felt I was dealt a lousy hand. I always questioned him. I allowed that particular animosity to control me and how I viewed things. God had it already planned out. He knew my parents weren't meant to be a union because He knew the environment wouldn't be healthy for none of us. What I needed was not to question His authority. I doubted Him and believed He had failed me. Still, I learned that He saved me from living with trauma that could have damaged my parenting abilities and how to maintain healthy relationships.

3rd Truth: I didn't understand who my dad was as an individual, but now I realize that he loved me to the best of his abilities and the only way he knew how. He was the best dad he could be in his eyes. My father has apologized several times for his actions, and we have had family mediation, which I acknowledged then. We have had some positive moments and some infuriating ones. In these times, my siblings have expressed their feelings about our relationship. Still, please understand each family has their dysfunction, and this just so happened to be ours. One of the Ten Commandments states, "Honor thy father and mother." I was wrong for allowing my pain to fester for years; it was up to me to stop internalizing my true feelings and let them be clear and heard. Dad, you hurt me to the core, yet I still respect and love you unconditionally. I am not saying that my actions or some of my behaviors didn't cause this, but I am saying that I was broken and misunderstood. It was hard to let go of the past, and the longer I held on to it, I suffered and experienced pain. I didn't know how to forgive in these moments because I couldn't forget. Until one day, I woke up with my dad heavy on my heart. I picked up the phone and said, "Daddy, I love you. Although it hurt, I no longer want to carry this emotional burden, and I forgive you."

4th Truth: I didn't know who I was. My teenage years were so conflicted that I allowed so much to be taken away from me that overflowed into adulthood, from the neglect of my self-esteem, self-worth, confidence, integrity, and intelligence to be challenged. I was damaged on the inside, and I walked around with this facade as if I had it all together. I was striving for acceptance, but during these moments, I was letting myself down each time because I was pleasing people. When in fact, I should have been focused on myself. I failed myself and allowed the perception of others to become my reality, including my father's opinion.

5th Truth: Going to prison saved my life. God knew I no longer needed to be a prisoner of my past. He knew that I would never focus on myself if I remained free. So, he sat me down to reveal my opportunities for change and growth. I was weak and had to sit with myself to become in touch with my inner soul. I had to be delivered from those broken fragments of hurt and jealousy of trying to fit in that resided in my heart. I had to change the narrative of my life. I needed to be challenged. He knew the only way to do that was to follow the 3Rs and **REMOVE** everything away from me, including my family, possessions, and career. **REVEAL** my failures, with the choices I made to myself, and **REPLACE** Faith back into my heart and belief that He has me no matter what it looks like.

The heart of the matter is...

The truth that matters most is that God created me to stand out. My life wasn't designed to have a place anywhere but in His hands. He loves me unconditionally, and loving myself hasn't always been key. I had allowed my mind to be compromised. I needed to learn how to tell my story without reliving the moment I once was in. I needed to become my number one fan. I am the star of my movie, and my storyline is only defined by God and me.

From my healing heart to your hurting heart, God made me an outcast the moment I was born. I just had to learn how to live life without man's acceptance.

You may never get the level of what you're looking for to the magnitude you desire. But he makes no mistakes in our trials and tribulations. Life isn't a playground, but it is a classroom. The journey through our lives is provided by tests needed for our growth and development.

Fragments of a Heart That Never Cried

Alva Pope

I stay busy. It's my thing; it's my coping mechanism because I don't want to feel what I feel and have known my entire life. I don't fit in; I'm not designed to fit in. And while most would probably revel in this notion and believe that this sounds good, it is a very lonely place to be. Honestly, I haven't felt this sad and heartbroken in twenty-five years.

I don't want to feel this.

If I feel it, it will devour me.

I feel like the disparity of it will choke me and break me down.

But I refuse to cry.

In fact, the last time I did was when my mother died two weeks after my youngest daughter was born. Other than that, I have not allowed myself to feel anything that deeply. The level of vulnerability needed to produce tears, well, frankly, I don't have time for it. But don't misunderstand me; I am human. I have the scars to prove it. And that is the issue…my scars. I am a grown woman with a thousand cuts to my soul.

My earliest memories of the initial cuts started when I was a kid. I had to fight for the right to be me amongst my siblings. I use the word fight because that's what I felt I had to do; otherwise, my identity, the real me, would have been lost forever. Amongst the snares and snide remarks, today's terminology is shade I received from my sisters was relentless. I was taunted for things I should have been celebrated for, like being a straight-A student. They acted as if I had received some gift, or family gene, that they didn't get. Yeah, what I got was the cut of isolation and spending time alone; it was difficult to be where I was unwanted. But I found things to do, be good at, and stay out of everybody's way. Their recognition of my presence and accomplishments grew more viscous as I grew older, always laced with put-downs. "Oh, look at big head; she's so smart." A huge part of me felt the need to downplay my academic acumen instead of embracing it. It was just another cut at my identity – be anyone except Alva. Don't ask questions; for goodness' sake, don't act like you know anything they don't know.

I was baffled, and because rejection had become a constant and consistent companion, I faced its slashes often. I was in Mr. Clarke's 4th-grade class when he decided to make a spectacle out of me. Mr.

Clarke was a prideful man, well put together. He did not like any student who was smarter than his son, especially not an inner city, uncultured, poor student like me. I hated it when anyone acted like being from the inner city made you dumb. I was well-known for my academic accomplishments, and most teachers liked me. Then, on a random day in his class, he said, "Let's see how smart you really are. I am going to give you an assignment. And I would like you to follow the directions on the front. Let's see if you are as smart as you think you are." I knew he was referring to me. I was cut again. He provided the handout to us, placing it face down on our desks. I read the sheet, and there were more than 50 questions. I immediately picked up my pencil and started to work. The directions simply stated: read every line before you start. I thought I have got to prove that I am smart enough." I rushed through, answering as many questions as I could. Frantic, trying to prove that I was worthy of my accomplishments, trying to prove that I had earned the title of scholastic standout. It was all I had, and no one was taking it from me. Mr. Clarke called time, but I wasn't finished. I was defeated. And the insult to this major injury was his final statement, "Maybe you aren't that smart. If you'd followed directions, you would have known that all you were required to do was sign your name." I still did not cry. Not immediately. I refused.

I graduated high school at seventeen. I had a boyfriend – with a sixth-grade education level. He was abusive because he'd been shamed and made to feel bad about himself. I was preparing for college and had tired of his tactics. The days of puppy love had withered and had been replaced with criticism, comparison, and violence. I was no longer enamored with ideas of chastity and him being my one and only. I was tired of the bickering that turned into a slap here and a punch there. He'd always been a bully and had a habit of forcing his will and way upon me. Once, he held me down and forced himself on me. I never reported it because I could not readily prove it. I broke it off with him. However, my mom got sick and was hospitalized, and I had to return home briefly after starting college. He found me and forced his way inside my car. Despite my pleading, he would not get out. This part is hard to explain, but this interaction was under duress. He had threatened to kill me before when I refused his advances. But this time, I was afraid. Afraid for everybody. I'd made it, and here he was, pulling me back. When I merged onto the highway, traveling at 60 mph, he turned the car off. Just deaded the engine. I was furious, worried about my mom, worried about school, and tired. The car choked, sputtered, and slowed down. It was late, and there was little traffic. But we fought. I mean, I fought, and I fought hard. I punched him in his face with enough force to bust his lip wide open. I restarted the car and regained control of an out-of-control situation. There was no room for tears; I did not cry. I did not have time for it.

I learned to fight from that day forward because I had to; otherwise, my own fear would choke the life out of me. Others had not chosen to do right by me, but I would always choose myself. And when I suspect or detect the slightest hint of exclusion, regardless of the messenger, it is met with my own heat: screw you, yeah fuck all of you! Digging my hands further into more open wounds, my insides scream, "I don't need your help; I can figure it out myself." I get frustrated when I collide with people, especially those I like, who make their ignorance painfully clear by asking veiled questions about my intelligence. "Who wrote this? Who helped you write this?" While denying the pit in my stomach and ignoring my inner warrior, my inward response is I did motherfu##er. Of course, my outward responses are always appropriate and mostly politically correct. But, it was not until now that I realized the impact these interactions have had on my perception and acceptance of myself.

The heart of the matter is...

I would have initially told you that these interactions with my siblings, teachers, and boyfriend didn't matter. But I now realize that I'd be test-a-lying, diminishing and denying my cuts, my wounds, my pain, and mostly, my tears. I have recalled these stories before and had dressed them up nice and pretty for presentation purposes. But now, these memories challenge me collectively, mostly in ways that I don't like. I'm just now realizing that these experiences have perpetuated issues plaguing my life. I have had many opportunities to sit with my thoughts, befriend my intelligence, and reflect on myself. Instead of enjoying my personality, I have questioned myself based on the responses of others, their avoidance, and their rejection of me. I have questioned my presence, inclusion, or exclusion from certain events or activities. And I have questioned my worth and value based on other people's ideas, opinions, and feedback. And I believed the problem was me.

But, **the truth of the matter is** I am an eternal verity. I am my own truth. I have now given myself permission to accept my experiences as personal and unverifiable. No other person on this planet can live my truth, and therefore no one can disapprove or prove me. I was born with my gifts and my talents, and I no longer seek approval for them. Everything I share in this chapter is a part of the fragments of my heart. Each devastating detail has presented me with this choice: do I agree with this, or is there something better? I have learned to honor the authenticity of my journey. The facts, the fear, the fragments, and the judgment of them all. I have allowed the opinions of others to decorate my responses and behavior for far too long. And I am no better because of it. I am no wealthier, no more included than I have been in the past, nor am I more accepted by others. And, no, I have not cried. I have stayed busy. And despite my toughness and refusal to cry, I believe in tears. And I believe that weeping is a valuable expression of life. However, life has taught me that vulnerability costs a lot. In fact, sharing your sorrows with the wrong people could cost you your life, literally.

From my healed heart to your hurting heart...

I continue on my journey, moving swiftly and steadily, seeking safety. I dedicate my life to creating this safety for others, making sure that they don't have to run and hide because vulnerability costs too much. I hold space for others and for me. I am a collector of tears because I understand their value. In fact, the tears that I have not yet shed are being collected. I collect my tears for my mother and my daughters, who reflect all the love that I could ever possess. I collect my tears for my siblings, who were too busy hiding their own pain that they released it by rejecting me. I collect my tears for the prideful teacher that misunderstands his privilege of guarding the gifts of children in his care. I collect my tears for those boyfriends that have been shamed and only feel powerful when their shame is used to bully those that care for them. I collect my tears for myself because I have rejected my own power and endured a thousand cuts to my soul. And when I am ready, I shall weep day and night.

Fragments of a Whole Heart

A Fresh Perspective on Brokenness

Tabatha Dandridge

My breath escaped my lips like a rushing wind when I checked the time on my worn straight talk flip phone and thought, when are you going to get another phone? I chuckled but quickly recalled the day Evan threw my blackberry on the floor, breaking it when I threatened to call the police when he wouldn't leave my apartment on the south side of town; the flip phone I'd kept as a backup when I'd gotten the blackberry. My eyes darted to the three holes he'd left in the walls when I kicked him out months earlier. I really hated looking at those holes; they reminded me of how petrifying that night had been. Those could have been blows to my face. It's bizarre, really. Those holes, in many ways, mirrored how I saw myself, empty, worthless, bare, and insubstantial. I'd often considered fixing them but figured it would be too expensive as I was living off unemployment and barely making rent. Besides, they had become a part of my norm, a part of my existence, a part of the deficits in my life that caused me to

104

wonder if this void, this emptiness I felt, was all my life would ever be.

Exasperated, I looked back at my cell phone. I would leave soon to meet Chase, an old acquaintance. I opened my fridge and pulled out the forty I'd purchased earlier in the day just for this occasion. I knew I would need a buzz before I saw him. Chase stood about 5'10, skinny, with caramel skin and brown eyes; he was a nice dude, but he wasn't someone I was interested in; besides, he was in a relationship and best friends with the man I once thought I'd marry. That fact alone should have repelled me, but it didn't. I was in the I don't give a fuck phase, and Chase was just another fuck nigga to me. So, in some ways, my getting with him was revenge on his bitch ass friend who had betrayed me.

Twisting off the cap, I took it straight to the head and wished I had a blunt; three hits, just three hits, and this forty would get me all the way right! Glancing at my phone again, I got in my Jeep and drove a few blocks until I reached the dimly lit parking lot of the motel. Overwhelmed, I blinked fast and hard to dry up the tears threatening to roll down my face. I knocked on the door, and Chase greeted me as I entered.

"Hey, Boy," I said. To the right, I saw the small but sufficient makeshift bar. There were brown and white liquors, ice, two glasses, soda, and juice to mix it. Chase was a drinker, for sure. He poured my first glass, looking on as I downed it, and then poured myself another. "Slow down before you get sick," I said, but I didn't listen; actually, I didn't care. Girl, you are so stupid! Why are you playing the ho' for this dude? You so dumb. You're better than this. So I thought, but I kept drinking. Then, after a while, I noticed the bottle was almost empty. "Damn, Tab, you drank all of that?" I blurted out. Yet, the buzz I wanted, anticipated, and desperately sought eluded me.

Later that night, Chase confessed he'd had a crush on my sister when we were younger. I looked at him in total disgust. Like, dude, really. You and your saggy balls. How could you lay here with me, having had a thing for my sister? I started to get in my feelings, but that would make me a hypocrite, considering he was best friends with the guy I'd dated ten years prior. Besides, I didn't like him like that, nor did my sister.

Sleeping with Chase did not diminish the feelings of loneliness that prompted me to accept his invitation to meet in the first place. Instead, it was almost like an out-of-body experience - like I was watching myself perform. I'd buried my face in the pillow as if that would somehow cause me to disassociate with what this loneliness, this hurt, caused me to do and feel.

I felt the presence of this thing. This thing had been following me for years. But I'd never felt the weight of its presence as much as I did this night. It covered me like a weighted blanket but provided no comfort. Instead, it invoked fear, yet I couldn't stop what I was doing. I felt like prey being hunted, much like a mythical vampire. He had finally caught me, sinking its fangs into the very vein of my soul, draining me of life's hopes and dreams. I wondered what death would be like. Would this thing drain every drop of it, or would it stop short of taking my life, causing me to awaken to the realization I'd morphed into the very thing I was running from...brokenness.

After a few hours, I dressed and headed for the door, but Chase stopped me. I didn't want to be there, he was just a tool I used to combat the emptiness, yet he convinced me to stay the night. It all seemed twisted at the moment. However, it fed my need to be wanted. Sleep wouldn't find me. I was restless. My brain was constantly bombarded with questions I had no rational answers for. I desperately sought to make sense of what I knew was complete and utter foolishness. My mind raced; you are really fucked up to do some shit like this. "I know I am," I whispered. "I know."

In the morning, as I walked to my vehicle, thinking, were you so starved for attention that you had to get with this man? At that moment, I felt like the lady in the scarlet letter; the label whore was pinned on me, and I knew for sure everyone could see my shame. I vowed to take what happened in that hotel room to the grave; it was just another skeleton in the closet threatening to encapsulate me. Why would you subject yourself to this? A slurry of questions started again, causing my head to hurt. This new secret added more turmoil; it left me spiraling further into this pit of worthlessness. I had, for sure, succumbed to a new low. You played yourself, and this episode would be just another screwed-up occurrence in your life. I drove away, stunned that I had consumed almost a whole bottle of liquor, a forty, and never got sick. Damn, you a G Tab. You a G! Bursting into spontaneous laughter, I turned the Go-Go music up high, my laugh dissipating as fast as it started. "Nah," a voice said, "You're just crazy as hell!" That experience was one of many questionable life decisions that left me pondering: was I the greatest or the craziest?

A move to Missouri (then back to Virginia) sometime later uncovered a stronghold of rejection. While unpacking rejection and its attributes, I realized its role in my health. While my self-esteem and worth needed more work - I was doing better than in previous years. Still, I needed to pinpoint the fragmented area that threatened to keep me on a carousel. I was in a constant cycle of meeting people, having an expectation of them but not having one for myself. I wanted to be seen positively, yet, I wasn't seeing myself that way. While at the PX, I recall some prominent women in ministry stopped by the booth where I worked. We knew each other as our paths often crossed due to different church functions and them being friends with my pastors. As the conversation unfolded, an overwhelming feeling of inadequacy came over me. I had no business engaging with them; they couldn't possibly want me in their conversation. So, on the inside, I began to shrink. These women spoke publicly on well-known platforms, and here I was little ole me. I felt so small and insignificant next to them. Finally, the revelation came flooding in; rejection had left fragments of a broken spirit, a poor self-image, and unworthiness.

Until then, I hadn't seen the connection between brokenness and wholeness. The process of undoing to become. If I am to stand in my authentic truth, it wasn't any one thing, experience, or incident that brought me to this place; it was a collection of it all. I had to allow the truth to tear down the stronghold of facts. The common denominator in my life story is me. I held a defeatist attitude, thinking my life wasn't worth anything. To change, I had to acknowledge and take ownership of the events in my life. I was so busy protecting others I had forgotten to protect myself. It doesn't eschew the fact that others influenced my perception of me. Still, at what point would I stand up and take ownership of how I was allowing people to treat me and how I was treating myself.

The heart of the matter is...

As I write this chapter, I must confess my transparency says I'm not sure this is the right piece, story, or episode of my life to reveal. There are many major moments, mistakes, and occurrences that are just as significant that have given me a hard shake, which shifted the trajectory of my perspectives and actions. When I became tired of just existing and drifting through life with a, whatever happens, happens mentality; I determined I wanted more. I wanted to live from a place of victory, not defeat. Each awakening and each paradigm shift brought me closer to that goal. It requires me to show up for myself daily, working to uncover what it means to be whole, walk in purpose, and discover myself. It took a milestone birthday for me to realize I didn't love myself. Not that I wasn't aware in some ways, but now I truly recognize it and give it a voice. That came with understanding and acknowledgment. I was showing up for everyone else, and I had to ask myself, when are you going to show up for yourself?

I've discovered brokenness doesn't mean I'm devoid of wholeness. It simply means there are area's where I must awaken to my potential. That awakening comes from tearing down the narrative of facts and shifting my mindset and perspective toward truth. That truth may require training, therapy, courses, mentorship, or a combination of those things. It definitely requires my vulnerability and intentionality, and I would be remiss if I left out my faith. It's been the anchor to the very core of who I am. My faith teaches me that in Jesus, there is nothing broken and nothing missing. Missing means nothing lacking. I have been given all the necessary tools, weaponry, giftings, talents, and ability needed to reach the desired goal God has for me. It is not His will that I cruise through life aimlessly. He is a God of intentionally, and He created me with a purpose in mind. I am determined to discover what that purpose is. My faith also teaches me that I am in Him, and He is in me. He is complete. Therefore, I must be. His grace covers my mistakes, and His love is beyond measure. I am accepted in the beloved, meaning He loves me unconditionally. His narrative of me is absolute, not man's narrative or life's experiences that have caused me to adopt a different narrative from His.

So I had to come alive to that truth: Nothing lacking, missing, or broken. That I am whole and complete in Him. When joined together, all the fragments, life experiences, successes, and failures make up a whole me! Like a puzzle, I took one piece or area of my life at a time and discovered where or

111

how the pieces fit. Sometimes I get it right off the bat, and other times, well, it takes unlearning and coming to terms with some things about myself. Sitting in the pain of an experience and uncovering the lesson. Speaking well over myself and forgiveness. Now that one… that one right there is crucial. I found there truly is a release that comes with forgiveness. It's not for the other person or letting them off the hook per se, but I actually felt the weight of its release because I took back my energy. I was devoting time to the offense, yet I've discovered that forgiveness clears my mind, thoughts, and heart for what's coming, allowing God's glory to flow into my life. Besides, I've found that most times, those people have gone on living their lives. Whether I cross their minds or not is none of my business. I'm just grateful God delivered me from dysfunction and the parts I played in my hurt. I had to acknowledge those flawed areas, patterns, triggers, and behaviors that undermined my growth. It wasn't easy looking at myself; I cried over the distress I allowed myself to experience. I even apologized to myself for the places I never should have gone, for not protecting me, for not setting boundaries, or for not staying committed to the boundaries I set. I have since promised myself to bring me into spaces that cause me to grow, thrive, and be safe. To allow my heart to be open to love and that love flows unhindered to others, especially me.

Learning to love me has been priceless. The joy that comes as a result of it is indescribable.

From my healed heart to your hurting heart: Achieving wholeness is possible. It won't be easy, as it will require intentionality. You must be committed to the process and extend grace to yourself. Take a moment to assess where you are in your journey, decide where you want to be, and shift your perspective on that area of brokenness by focusing on wholeness and what that looks like for you. Align yourself with what God's Word says about it and take the necessary steps. Again, imploring commitment, intentionality, and grace. You won't get there overnight, but if you keep going, I believe you will.

Now What?

What you read is the manifestation of twelve hearts beating simultaneously through hurt, brokenness, insecurity, unacceptance, and fear. You witnessed scattered fragments being weaved back together through tears, perseverance, persistence, and faith. As you turned each page, you may have paused to wipe away tears while recalling or reliving moments in your life journey. Perhaps you were stuck on a particular chapter as you realized the pain you tried so hard to suppress never left. The shame and doubt you fought hard to put behind you resurfaced and came tumbling down. And much like Humpty Dumpty, you found yourself staring at broken pieces. Maybe the fragments of your heart are fresh, and now you're asking yourself, "What do I do with these shattered pieces?" The good news is that your heart is still beating, which means the fragments did not destroy you.

The book that you are holding is your first step toward healing. Wholeness is possible, but it can't be rushed. The writers have put in the work. They have remembered and re-experienced painful places they thought were forgotten or simply failed to confront.

This collaboration was birthed with healing in mind, not just for the writer, but for you - the reader. The chest pains that each writer endured were necessary and strategic. Every irregular palpitation was tolerated so that you would feel strengthened to confront the unhealthy conditions of your own heart. For every dis-ease that each writer faced, it was to challenge you to do your own wellness check and propel you to begin the removal process.

We encourage you to allow each chapter to recharge your life. You can't afford to leave the core of your being unattended any longer. Go deep into the heart of the matter until you dare to tell yourself the truth. Stay in tune with the beat of your heart and have the audacity to face the unhealthy triggers that causes it to skip a beat.

Your next step will require you to be intentional about dealing with the shattered pieces. The process can be challenging and scary, but the healing far exceeds the temporary pain. You owe it to yourself to treat the blockage and reset the rhythm of your heart.

But please! Don't try to take on your entire process at once. Start with one fragment, one step...one heart promise!

That's where we started.

115

My Heart Promise

I will no longer ignore the healing you crave. I will submit to the process that is required for you to freely forgive, embrace God's love, and finally accept that you have the right to experience uncompromised happiness. I will work daily to strengthen you and release the fragments that can no longer exist in this resuscitated vessel. I celebrate you for all that you have endured. The real promise is this...I promise to be healed and to use everything you've survived to help someone else who is struggling to mend the shattered pieces of their broken heart story.

—Ifedayo Greenway

Dear Heart,

I first want to apologize for putting other hearts before you. Please forgive me for ignoring your weight limit. From this day forward, I vow to put you first and give you my undivided attention. It's time for us to be whole!

—Jada D. Thompson

My Heart Promise is simply this - to take good care of those fragmented pieces that God has graciously restored. I promise to allow my heart to feel whatever it needs to feel. I also promise not to allow broken pieces to keep me from hearing the voice of God, even when I think God is silent or speaking just above a whisper.

—Sandra L. Parker

I promise never to allow anyone to humiliate me or make me feel less than others. I will never allow anyone to make me so angry that I question God's motives. Dear heart, I promise to make better decisions while loving you more.

—Felicia L. Vereen

Precious Heart. I cherish and honor you as you live in the freedom of your beauty. I will not allow others' expectations of you to diminish your greatness. I will boldly embrace our authentic love and encourage others to do the same. I will use our healing journey to help the broken-hearted to be seen and rest in the freedom of their being. Dear Heart, we are enough. We are perfect manifestations of God's Love.

—Mavis G. Rowe

My Heart Promise is to continue to make me proud by striving through my struggles, and persevering through the pivotal points of my life, while releasing the matters of my heart.

—Charita Waddy

Dear Heart,

- ❁ *I love you, and I am so proud of how you persevere through every trial and obstacle that comes your way. I promise I will take so much better care of you.*

- ❁ *I will not allow you to be burdened by offenses and the wrongdoing of others.*

- ❁ *Over the years, you've learned how to receive and give love. I will make sure you remain open to healthy love.*

117

❀ *No longer will fear or frailty rule over you.*

❀ *You endured so much in the most vulnerable stages of your life, but I promise you will use the wisdom and discernment you gained to lead you.*

—Tiffany M. Roberts

My dear heart, I promise to walk out this season of healing so you can finally be well. I vow to think more of you and the beats God allows to come through you to give me life. I will honor you now more than ever before. Forgive me for not making better choices outside of my pain. In spite of how I have ignored your throbbing signals and aching, you never have given up on me. You just keep on beating in sync with my breath giving me life. Thank you for being stronger for me than I have been for you. This time I will respect you and treat you better. You are my heart - you deserve it.

—Marcia L. Ali

My heart! I promise that I will continue to do the work and walk through the pain necessary to make you whole; I was going to say again, but I don't think you've ever been made whole. But, you will be as I walk through this process of revealing and healing. You will be made whole, and you will know that you are loved.

—Gwendolyn Winston-Marrow

I CHERON, will love you unconditionally, wholeheartedly. I will love you even when it gets uncomfortable.

I have failed you for over 30 years of my life. To the point that I tried to take my life because of what I thought I had to be for others. I was a coward to my feelings.

I promise to lean on God and understand His direction is a protective mechanism. I promise to "Trust the Process". Lastly, I promise to never stop removing the fragments and layers of a conflicted heart to fuel a more healthier one!

—Cheron Johnson

I promise to honor my heart. It is truly the center of my life. I commit to creating a space of safety for my own heart. Love is the evidence of the presence of God in my life and because I'm always with God, I am safe. I give myself permission to let my tears flow.

—Alva Pope

My heart's promise is to love you, Tabatha. I commit to putting in the work to bring you to a place where you feel safe, seen, and appreciated. Where you walk in the light of what God intended for you...wholeness - nothing missing, nothing broken. I'm not saying you'll never have tests or trials, but rather, I'm committed to getting and implementing the tools necessary to guard your heart, yet, allow love to flow through it unhindered so that the glory on the inside will manifest effectively on the outside.

—T.L.Dandridge

My Heart Promise - Call to Action

Perhaps, one of the most important decisions and promises you can make relative to your heart is to accept our Heavenly Father and invite Him into it.

I read somewhere that the only one who can truly satisfy the human heart is the person who made it.

You've read our stories. They are a clear indication that perfection is not a requirement to be in covenant with God. In fact, a relationship with Him means you get to come to the table just as you are. He wants your deep heart. The center of you that is the truest part of you. He's waiting with open arms. He wants a relationship with the REAL YOU! Will you trust Him with all of your pieces and give Him your heart today?

> *"For it is by believing in your heart that you are made right with God, and it is by openly declaring your faith that you are saved."* Romans 10:10 (NLT)

About
The Authors

Ifedayo Greenway

Ifedayo Greenway is a mother, speaker, and master life coach.

She is the CEO of IG & MORE LLC. As a transformational coach, Ifedayo produces an annual event, The Change Experience, which empowers women to embrace their personal change journey.

She is the founder of the She Unveils movement where she serves and helps others accomplish their literary goals through unveiling, writing, and publishing their stories. She has been featured in Huffington Post, CBS, FOX, NBC, and Shoutout Atlanta for her literary works (Removing The Face & Removing The Fear).

Ifedayo is a six-time author & three-time best-selling author. Other published works include inspirational writings and articles that have reached thousands of readers in various mediums including Thrive Global & Faith Heart Magazine.

Ifedayo is passionate about her covenant with God to impact the world & uses her journey to strengthen & encourage women to find their authentic voice in their pursuit of transformation.

Connect with Ifedayo at:
www.igandmore.com

Jada D. Thompson

Jada D. Thompson was born in Albany, Georgia and raised in Chesapeake, Virginia. She is the oldest daughter of Tahisha P. Thompson and the Unforgettable Nelson J. Thompson. Jada has one younger sister, Jami'yah Thompson, who is her best friend. Jada is a graduating senior at Norfolk State University majoring in Interdisciplinary Studies and minoring in Psychology.

Jada is the founder of Gracefully Broken Prophetic Ministries, where she specializes in Worship & Arts, public speaking, and mentoring. Her passion is to bridge the gap in relationships between fathers and daughters. After suddenly losing her father at the age of seventeen, she became an advocate for daughters who have lost their beloved fathers. Her loss caused her to embrace those who suffer with loss and the weight of grief from themselves and others.

Connect with Jada at:
2jadamay@gmail.com

Sandra L. Parker

Sandra L. Parker is the founder and visionary of Speak Life on Purpose, LLC., a movement designed to empower women to embrace a "think different, speak different" mindset.

Focusing on her life experiences, Sandra encourages women to embrace change and access their power to grow. She has a strong desire to see women turn their pain into positive growth. As a mindset coach, she aims to help women move from a fixed mindset to a growth mindset.

Sandra believes that God's mandate as it concerns women is to encourage, motivate and inspire them to demolish old mindsets and to provide them with affirming tools that empowers them to use their authentic voice to Speak Life over every area of their lives regardless of their circumstances.

Sandra is a mother of one daughter, a licensed minister, a certified professional life and mindset coach, a two-time best-selling author, and a transformational speaker.

Connect with Sandra at:
www.speaklifeonpurpose.org

Felicia L Vereen

Felicia L. Vereen is the author of ROCK Your Money, co-author of Today I Choose Me and co- founder of InspireHer the Total Woman Podcast. She is a mother, financial coach, and motivational speaker. Felicia is a Richmond, Virginia, native and holds a Master's in Business Administration from Averett University and a Bachelor of Science in Accounting from Norfolk State University.

She has served Corporate America for over 20+ years working in the financial industry and has worked for several Fortune 500 companies. Felicia's personal finance expertise and love for financial literacy have helped her partner with several organizations including Empowering a Billion Women (EBW), Contributor to James Malinchak's "Live Your Passion" book project, and several other speaking engagements. When she is not speaking or coaching Felicia aims to make a difference in the community by using her unique gift for making the complicated clear.

Connect with Felicia at:
FVereen@gmail.com

Mavis G. Rowe

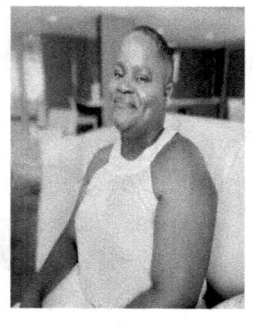

Mavis G. Rowe is a native of Portsmouth, VA. Her motto is "If you don't like something, change it. If you can't change it, change your attitude."-Maya Angelou. Mavis is a licensed clinical social worker who currently works with the geriatric community. She holds a master's degree in social work from Norfolk State University and a master's in divinity from Virginia Union University. She's passionate about empowering women to be mentally, physically, and spiritually whole and specializes in grief and mental wellness. Mavis is a proud wife and mother of 6 adult children. She's a member of The Mount at Chesapeake and is involved with the Counseling Ministry. She's an Amazon Bestselling author with her participation in "Removing the Fear: A Truth Journey from Fear to Freedom".

Her first solo work "They're Gone. Now What?: A Grief Journey from Self-torment to Soul-Transformation" was released in 2022.

Connect with Mavis at:
www.m.rowe.lcsw@gmail.com

Charita Waddy

Charita Waddy is the founder of WHAM (What About Me) an organization geared toward promoting one to love yourself for who you are today while bettering you for tomorrow.

Charita is a woman of many talents where she attended Highland Springs Technical Center for (cosmetology), Strayer University (Business Administration, and SNHU (Health Administration). She takes pride in pursuing her mission to help others see the beauty of self by creating events in a safe space that allows one to share their everyday struggles of life that holds them back from being their best self. Allowing GOD to direct her path, Charita strives to implement the word through her everyday walks of life.

She is native of Richmond, Virginia, and a mother of one daughter, one son, and grandmother of one.

Her motto of life is **"You're never too old to learn, nor too young to teach" so "Live to learn, while learning to live".**

Connect with Charita at:
whamwhataboutme@gmail.com

Tiffany M. Roberts

Tiffany Roberts is an advocate for healing and restoration for at risk troubled girls and women who have suffered abuse of any form. Through her own life's obstacles and proven resiliency, she finds joy in strengthening others to overcome and walk in God's calling for their lives. She is a fitness enthusiast who, through her own experience with diabetes, has publicly spoken to audiences while also serving as a "behind the scenes" health coach for people suffering with chronic illnesses. Professionally, she has held leadership positions in the banking, technology and investment industry. She takes her relationship with God seriously and is called to serve as Deaconess at her church. As a proud wife, she has a blended family of four adult children and four grandchildren. Through her transparency, it is her dream to help others reach their full potential.

Connect with Tiffany at:
tiffmoni95@gmail.com

Marcia L. Ali

Marcia L. Ali is a family advocate affectionately known as Auntie757 and Teenologist. Marcia is a speaker, business owner and two time bestselling author who is souled-out for teens. Marcia is a licensed Behavioral Health nurse and Peer Recovery Specialist. Marcia is the founder of the non-profit T.O.F.T. (Time Out for Teens). Her desire for seeing teens "be great" comes from her personal experience with her son being sentenced to eighteen years in a New Jersey state prison when he was 18 years old. Marcia works to pull greatness out of every teen she encounters. Marcia is known for her motherly wisdom and has the gift of bridging the gaps of broken mother/daughter relationships.

Marcia is a native of Newark, New Jersey. Marcia is a wife, mother and grandmother residing in Suffolk, Virginia. Marcia truly believes that love always wins.

Connect with Marcia at:
marciaali757@gmail.com

Gwendolyn Winston-Marrow

Gwendolyn Winston-Marrow is the innovator and CEO for Gwen's Inspirational Moments, a platform that she uses to inspire and encourage others to keep moving forward. She has been married for over 40 years. She is a mother, grandmother and a powerful orator and workshop facilitator. For over 25 years Gwen has been facilitating powerful life changing workshops that exhort, encourage and empower others to be the motivational power that transforms their lives. She is passionate about restoration and healing in peoples' lives and uses the limpidity of her own life to prove that your place of pain can also become your place of power. She has ministered nationally and internationally and works diligently to fulfill her mission to help others to become the best person they can become so that they may be the best at whatever they have chosen to do in life.

She loves to bake and is well known for her cheesecake and pound cake; hence her business Gwen's Slice of Heaven. Everything she does she does in a spirit of excellence.

She attended Virginia State University, Virginia Commonwealth University and Fredericksburg Bible College. She was employed by the Department of Social Services and is a former Army Reservist.

Connect with Gwendolyn at:
gmarrow.gm@gmail.com

Cheron Johnson

Cheron Johnson is the Executive Director of Chapter 2 Ent, a nonprofit foundation that focuses on rehabilitation and repositioning for citizens returning to society from incarceration. She is a woman with a purpose and refuses to give up. Her passion was driven by being sentenced to 72 months of incarceration. Cheron knew that the day of her release would be the day she returned to the world with a stronger vision. She was determined to position herself as a motivational mogul in the community, speaking and lifting others as she climbed to the top.

A native of Detroit, MI, and mother of a handsome son, Cheron is also the founder of Chapter 2 Consulting, an organization that establishes business literacy within entrepreneurs seeking leadership and development.

Her motto in life and business is **"trust the process."**

Connect with Cheron at:
chapt2ent@gmail.com

Alva Pope

Alva Pope is a master communicator, writer and therapist who is affectionately called "The Grief-ologist" by those who are familiar with her work. Her passion for life has allowed her to work as a professional social worker and ordained Pastor. Alva established and developed Touchstone Counseling Services where she provides outpatient therapy, psychosocial education, energy healing and professional development. Touchstone's mission is to assist the self-identified student-teacher in reaching their goals and greatest potential. Alva believes that "one good conversation can change your life" and uses her gifts of quality time and compassion to engage you in life altering pursuits. She is newly married, a mother of two and welcomes her bonus children into her home. She is a native of Richmond and received all her formal education in Virginia. Alva's newest pursuit is podcasting, and she plans to initiate production in mid-2023.

Connect with Alva at:
www.touchstonerva.com

Tabatha L Dandridge

From a small town in Virginia, Tabatha has always wanted to make a difference. Seeing people win and overcome life's adversities is her passion. Tabatha was featured in Shout Out Atlanta as the owner of Dandridge Office Solutions a virtual assistant business as well as the visionary behind the movement; Powered for Change, a faith based platform helping you maximize life's adversities by using them as stepping stones for your God given potential. Tabatha is the youngest of her siblings and mother of one. A bit introverted yet adventurous, she faces challenges with faith and tenacity. Writing has often helped her deal with some of life's difficult challenges and knowing she can possibly encourage someone by sharing a period in her life that took faith, determination, consistency and grit to overcome brings hope to her heart.

Connect with Tabatha at:
hello@TabathaLorraine.com